Matthew 7:7

Ask and it will be given to you;
Seek and you will find;
Knock and the door will be opened to you.

CONTENTS

Introduction xiii

1 Welcome 1
2 Here I Am 5
3 God's Great Love 11
4 Trust in the Lord 23
5 Never Alone 35
6 Why Not? 43
7 The Call 49
8 A New World 59
9 Back in Africa 79
10 Hoping, Waiting and Praying 95
11 Letting Go Even More 105
12 It's Over 119
13 Do Not Be Afraid 125
14 The Good News 141
15 Our Mission Is On 149
16 Finding My Way Home 159

Acknowledgments 165
Bibliography 169

For
Dave, Tyler & Fiona

In Loving Memory of My Grandparents
Houston, Helen, Gerald & Juanita

INTRODUCTION

Who am I? More so, who am I for Him? That question burns inside of me. There is a song by Casting Crowns called "Who Am I." [1] This song came into my life as I was entering a heavy season. I recall listening to it over and over as I sought peace in a trying world. I have since listened to this song a thousand times. It asks the question that many of us find ourselves asking, "Who Am I?" It answers with three simple words that hold greater meaning than we can truly comprehend—I Am Yours. What does this tell me? It tells me that I can look to Jesus, regardless of absolutely anything in my life, and answer, I Am Yours.

Who am I? This one question is the reason I am writing to you. You who are reading these pages. For many years, there has been so much stirring inside of me. I have wondered how I could put it all into words. How I would have the courage to share it. Here is what I know, though. I am not the only one asking, Who Am I? There is a world full of people seeking the answer to this question.

The answer to this question—You are His. My prayer is for

---

[1] Mark Hall. "Who Am I." Track 4 on *Casting Crowns*. Mark A Hall and Steven Curtis Chapman. Provident Music Distribution, 2003, compact disc.

every person to know who they belong to. There is not one soul He does not seek. No soul is unwanted. As the Casting Crown song sings,

> "I am a flower quickly fading,
> here today and gone tomorrow,
> a wave tossed in the ocean,
> a vapor in the wind,
> still you hear me when I'm calling, Lord,
> you catch me when I'm falling,
> and you've told me who I am,
> I am yours." [2]

I have held these lyrics close to my heart. I need to be reminded that God knows me. And, because He knows me, I can boldly answer, I am Yours.

---

[2] Hall. "Who Am I."

ONE

Welcome

Are not five sparrows sold for two pennies? Yet not one of them is forgotten by God. Indeed, the very hairs on your head are all numbered. Don't be afraid; you are worth more than many sparrows.

—Luke 12:6-7

This is my story: a story of life's most challenging and joy-filled moments; a story of hope; a story of how God has worked in my life through the highs and lows; a story of God's grace and love; a story of the faith we can have through Him, even in a troubled world; and ultimately, a story of victory in Jesus.

We each have a story to tell of our time here on Earth. For a long time, God has been calling me to share mine. Many things have gotten in the way. Life has gotten in the way, excuses have gotten in the way, but mostly, fear. Fear has gotten in my way. Someone once told me I needed to get out of my own way. How true. Often, I get in the way of doing what I need to do, and in this case, what God calls me to do. It's time to get out of my own way and let God take over. It's time to allow Him to do what I can't do alone.

As I started this project, I felt unqualified. I love to write, but this felt too big for me to handle alone. Thankfully, God kept calling me. He kept working on my unbelieving heart. He reminded me over and over that he does not call the qualified; he qualifies the called. I don't have to be qualified to do this alone. I have Him. And with Him, anything is possible.

Not knowing how to begin, God told me to simply tell my

story. He told me to start from the beginning and share with others the things that have happened in my life. How He walked with me and carried me through some of my darkest hours; how He never left my side. He told me to share how even on the hardest, most difficult days to face, He lifted me out of bed and helped me put one foot in front of the other. He said, "Tell them that the strongest thing I taught you how to do was to lean on me. Tell them how you ran to me at the end of every day to find the refuge and peace that couldn't be found anywhere else. Tell them that it was in the darkness that you found me. There is where we found our deepest bond. It was there that you truly came to know me as your Heavenly Father. Tell them that it was when life had you hanging onto a thread at the end of your frayed rope that you could most clearly see me and how it was there that you would allow yourself to fall into my arms. Tell them how you learned to surrender your battles to me, how you sent me into war on your behalf, and how I victoriously fought for you. Tell them how I have been able to fill that emptiness inside of you that only I can."

I am going to tell my story with Him. Through God's grace, He will help me show how He has worked in my life. I pray that your heart will be open to allow Him to meet you wherever you are, that you will truly see Him and allow Him into the middle of your mess. Allow Him to rescue you as He did me. I pray that you will be able to fall into His arms and surrender control.

Regardless of my fear, I very much want to share my story. So often, in so many ways, God puts thoughts in my mind of stories I could share about how He has worked in my life. He has placed a deep desire on my heart to share Him with others—with you—so I am turning over the pen to His most capable hands.

> *Luke 12:6-7 says, "Are not five sparrows sold for two pennies? Yet not one of them is forgotten by God. Indeed, the very hairs on your head are all numbered. Don't be afraid; you are worth more than many sparrows."*

If you have ever felt insignificant or alone, know that the God of the heavens has his eye on you. How could he not see you if his eye is on every bird in the sky? I hope to show you through my story how valuable you are in the eyes of your Father.

When I think of heaven, I think of being home. I am sharing a story that has begun but is not yet finished. I am sharing how I have laughed and cried my way through this sweet life God has given me. How I am not alone, how He walks with me, how He never leaves me for even one second, how He is just a breath away, and how He is waiting and longing for his children to come home to Him.

TWO

Here I Am

So that Christ may dwell in your hearts through faith. And I pray that you, being rooted and established in love, may have power, together with all the Lord's holy people, to grasp how wide and long and high and deep is the love of Christ, and to know this love that surpasses knowledge, that you may be filled to the measure of all the fullness of God.

—Ephesians 3: 17-19

When I was a child, one of my favorite songs to sing at church was "Deep and Wide." [3] The chorus sings, "Deep and wide, Deep and wide, there's a fountain flowing deep and wide." There were hand motions that went with it, and we would sing it countless times. As an adult, I read Ephesians 3:17-19, and it takes on a whole new meaning. As a child, I did not fully comprehend what the fountain represented. There are many interpretations of the song. Now I know that the fountain is God, whose love runs "wide and long and high and deep." His love is deeper and wider than we can understand, and it continuously flows—for us.

I want to share a few things. First, I am a work in progress. I am imperfect. God has been at work in my life for a long time. In many ways, I think He is just starting a work in me. Ever so slowly, but in His time, He reveals my purpose. He shows me one little step at a time. He knows that is all I can handle. I have come to accept that I will be in a constant state of transformation until the day I go home to be with Him. There are times I wish I could see into the future. If I only knew what was to come. He reveals

[3] Sidney E. Cox. *Deep and Wide.* Ruth P. Overholtzer in Salvation Songs for Children No. Three, 1947.

only what He needs me to see, allowing me to see the gift it can be to leave my future in His hands.

Second, I have spent time in the valleys. I still do. While the valleys have been the toughest, most painful times of life, I've never lost the feeling that God was with me and that He could turn my pain into something beautiful. I do not believe God causes or brings pain into our lives. We live in a fallen and sinful world, and there will be trouble. However, God is always present. He is present on the good days, and He is present on the bad days. In all our days, all He wants is for us to invite Him in. I will share some of the times I have been in the valleys. I know that while they were difficult, God was intervening, molding, shaping, and even preparing me for something big. I have believed in God my entire life. I always knew He was with me, but in the valleys, I truly found Him for the first time and invited Him to come along with me to live each day.

I am not an expert in what I am going to share. I am a regular person and want to humbly share my life. I read the Bible, but I am not a master of theology. This book will not be a scholarly read. I like to keep things simple. My faith is built on God's words and perhaps more by my experiences when God's words have come alive in my life. The words I share come directly from my heart. I am who I am. I live to be as genuine as I can possibly be. I am unapologetically me because that is what others deserve. I feel things deeply. I cannot hear bad news and immediately turn to another topic without a second thought. I love people, especially those with a story to tell. As much as I can feel sadness, I also fully celebrate joy. I strive to show kindness to people. I desire to leave people better than when I found them. I love to laugh. I use humor to enjoy life and sometimes to cope with life. I don't always have it all together, rarely, in fact. My house is never show-worthy. I have a to-do list that never seems to be complete. I am awkward, my kids will confirm, and I am okay with that. I am many things, good and bad. I still have a lot of growing to do and always will. The pages that follow will reveal this.

I am beginning to understand what it means to share God with others and the importance and urgency of that. It's hard to live our lives like an open book. It's hard to reveal the messiness, but I think that is how we must live. We can't hide how God has helped us. We have to unmask the brokenness. We have to share it because there is someone who desperately needs to hear it.

I don't know what you have been through in your life. I want you to know that while my experiences have been hard, I in no way think that what I have been through is harder than what you have been through. Each of us has a story. I know many people who have experienced unfathomable loss and pain. You may be experiencing it right now. Life is not a competition. No matter what has come your way, I want each person to know they are not alone. Let's meet each other exactly where we are and live this life together.

I don't know if you know God or if you've accepted Him into your life. I don't know if you had Him in your life at some point, but the pain you've endured has caused you to drift away. Perhaps you are still trying to figure out how to completely turn your problems over to God. Maybe you are just getting to know Him, learning to lean on Him and trust His promises. My hope and prayer, no matter where you find yourself, is that you will find something here that will open Him up to you in a new way. That you will find a glimpse of the hope you've been seeking.

So, I invite you into my life. Let me warn you, it's not all pretty. Just because I am a Christian does not mean that I always handle myself gracefully. In fact, I've been known to kick and scream and cry my way through certain trials. I want to share my life with you, my real and raw life as it has happened. I want to be transparent about my weaknesses. I am human and will never be the poster child for handling a crisis. There are times I have handled things with composure. And there are times I have fallen apart and been unable to function. I still worry; I still sin; I still lack faith. I am not perfect, nor would I ever want to portray that image. I invite you to share in my struggles. I invite you to see how God has rescued me. I invite you to experience the joy and victory He has brought into my life. Each of our stories is unique, yet everyone holds a common thread—we all need Jesus. I am finding my way home.

THREE

God's Great Love

Though the mountains be shaken and the hills be removed, yet my unfailing love for you will not be shaken, nor my covenant of peace be removed, says the Lord, who has compassion on you.

—Isaiah 54:10

Let me start by filling in a few details of my life. I was born and raised in Indiana in a Christian family. My grandfather and his father were ministers. I was blessed to have a loving family all around. My parents, Bruce and Sue, my identical twin sister, Becky, and my younger brother, Josh, made up our family. We moved a couple of times during my adolescent years, and putting aside the challenges of that, life was normal. I went to college for business and met my future husband, Dave, who I married after graduation. I was happy to continue to live a simple midwestern life. I expected our future to play out the way I envisioned. We would spend our lives with family and friends, go to church, work hard, and grow a family. Stay on course, on my schedule. My life was in my hands. Faith was easy, and life was sweet. And the first few years as a married, adult woman, it was just that. After five years of marriage, we welcomed a baby boy, our son Tyler, in 1999. What a joy! Life seemed to be going as planned.

I would have never envisioned my life since those early years. This is how my story begins.

October 5, 2006, is a day that will remain with me throughout my days. It is a day that I found myself at my lowest and a day that something miraculous happened in my life. A truly defining moment. A day that God was so close to me, I felt I could reach out and touch Him. A day that I experienced the peace that passes all understanding that could only come from Him. It happened to me in one of my darkest and scariest hours. It is a priceless gift that will never fade. I want others to know this gift also awaits them.

I will begin by going back a few days. I had been to my doctor's office for a routine visit but was not feeling well. Home pregnancy tests were negative; however, the doctor thought my uterus seemed enlarged after an exam. She told me that home pregnancy tests can't always be trusted, and why don't I come back on Tuesday for an ultrasound to see what might be happening. She also sent me on my way with a pack of prenatal vitamins to get me started "just in case." She said all of this so calmly. Little did she know who she was dealing with here. Our son Tyler was seven, and we'd been hoping for another baby for some time. So, imagine putting all of the above ideas into this optimistic mind of mine and setting me loose over a long weekend. A reasonable person may have been able to keep things in perspective. Unfortunately, I am not always reasonable. I left that doctor's appointment on cloud nine, the excitement growing quickly inside me. I knew this was going to be our time.

That following Tuesday, Dave joined me for the ultrasound, where we hoped to hear the news we'd been praying for. During the ultrasound, though, nothing could be found, except for the observation that my ovaries "looked old." After another pregnancy test, the nurse stopped in the room where we sat and told us, "It's negative, but keep trying." I managed to make it out of there, even smiling at the receptionist on my way. I reached the car and sat there in disbelief. I was inconsolable; there was such sadness in my heart. I felt such loss for something that never was; the hope for a child that had started growing in my heart long before this day.

Not only was I sad, I was also angry. How could I have been so naive? How could I ignore those home pregnancy tests? How could I once again hope for what would not happen? I was angry with myself. To be honest, I was angry with God too. How could God let me get my hopes up like that when He knew what the answer would be?

Emotionally exhausted, I made it through the rest of the week. That Saturday, we had plans to go out of town with some friends to a marriage seminar. While I was sad, we hoped it would be a way to find some distraction from our reality and relax. That afternoon, Tyler had a soccer game. I don't remember if they won or lost. I only remember how cold and rainy it was as I sat huddled under an umbrella, how I still did not feel right, and how heartbroken I had become. Regardless, we were determined to forge ahead with our evening. After his game, we got ready and headed out. We drove for a couple of hours and then stopped for dinner before the event. I started feeling worse as the hours passed. By the time we reached the event, I was starting to have some abdominal pain. I spent most of the evening pacing the halls and running to the bathroom. I was miserable on the drive home and prayed that I would not get sick in our friend's car. All I wanted was to get home, get into my bed, and try to shake this off.

Over the coming days, I experienced what I thought was the worst stomach flu of my life. I was running a high fever; everything was spinning around me. I had extreme abdominal pain and could not keep anything down. Looking back, I think I knew something was very wrong, but I didn't want to see it. This did not feel like any stomach flu I had ever experienced. On Sunday night, I left my boss a message saying I was hoping for a miracle, but without one, I would not be at work the next day. Monday was worse. That night, my frequent trips to the bathroom we unsuccessful. Thinking I must be severely dehydrated from being so sick, I continued to hope it was a really awful case of the flu. Tuesday, things were still not improving. That afternoon, I finally called my doctor's office and explained what was happening. The nurse quickly called back and said the doctor wanted me to head to the ER. She told me everything was probably okay, but the ER could work more quickly to get blood work done.

Things did not move quickly at the ER. We sat for what felt like forever. Finally, I had blood drawn and was sent to an exam room. They started a catheter to relieve my bladder. They also started me on IV fluids and gave me some pain medicine. As I started feeling some relief, things kicked into high gear. My blood work was back, and the ER staff came to tell me they were moving me to another exam room, which I later learned was the critical unit of the ER. I was immediately hooked up to a heart monitor and given a large cup of liquid potassium to drink. They sent me for a CT scan to see if they could find out what was going on inside of me. Meanwhile, they continued to add bags of medication to my IV pole.

My family doctor, who had sent me to the ER about that time, appeared in the doorway. He was a nice man and always greeted me with a warm smile. This day was different. He looked somber. He came to my side and explained that my white blood cell count was critically high and my potassium was so low they were concerned about my heart. The CT scan showed extensive inflammation in my entire abdominal area. An infection was raging through my body. And—I was in renal failure. Every word my doctor said seemed to hang in the air as I tried to process it. They knew all of this but had no idea what was causing it nor how to stop it. He told me to plan on at least a few days in the hospital as they tried to figure things out.

The next two days were some of the most challenging of my life. I was completely restless in every way possible. I was in tremendous pain, and nothing provided any comfort. My mind and body were at war. It felt impossible to find any relief or rest. The doctors pumped my body as full as possible with antibiotics to fight the infection attacking me. Even so, nothing was improving. IVs were blowing, and new ones were started. My veins could not keep up. Because of this and the immediate need to get the medicine in my body, a nurse told me they wanted to start a PICC line. I asked what that was, and she explained they would send a team to place a long tube in my arm in a larger vein traveling to my heart. I didn't like the sound of that, but having no choice, I agreed.

This was my third day in the hospital, October 5, 2006. The hospital was overloaded with patients and short on staff, so I shared a room with an older lady named Mary Jane. Mary Jane had an IV placed in the inner part of her elbow, which meant she needed to keep her arm straight or her IV pump would start beeping. Mary Jane had an awful time keeping her arm straight. She seemed oblivious to the loud beeping. All night I buzzed the nurses about Mary Jane's beeping IV. There was a drape between us, so I could not see her, but I found myself hollering to her in the night to please straighten her arm. I was desperate to find a hint of peace, and her IV was pushing me beyond my limits.

Even with that drape, Mary Jane knew I was there too. I had the bed by the window, so I had to walk by her anytime I needed to make a trip to the bathroom. I carried my catheter and an IV pole in each hand, carefully and slowly making my way to the bathroom while trying to keep my gown closed. I was not successful, and I am sure she was a witness to that a time or two. Bless her heart.

When the PICC line crew arrived, there were four of them. Each one had a lot of equipment, which they managed to fit into the little space that remained. This is where they would do the procedure. They sealed off my half of the room, but Mary Jane and her visitors remained on the other side of the curtain. A maintenance man in my room was replacing the oxygen tank above my head on the wall. He and his drill were hard at work, adding to the noise that was building. The crew finally asked him to leave, and he was none too pleased with the interruption. So, everything was set, and we were off. My mom was there, and I asked if she could stay. They agreed, but she turned white at the first sight of blood and was escorted to the hall to get some air. It took some time, but once the PICC line was in, they tidied up and were out of there in a flash.

They were barely out the door when my heart started

fluttering. Something was not right. The more it fluttered, the more I worried. I buzzed the nurse back into the room. They sent a tech with an x-ray machine to the room to check on the placement of the PICC line. He discovered that the line had been placed a little too close to my heart and was, as they put it, tickling it. It did not feel like a tickle; it felt like my heart was about to jump out of my chest!

The crew returned to my room and pulled the PICC line out a little, so it was no longer tickling my heart. By now, I was a wreck and having an awful time calming down. I had been pushed to what felt like my absolute limits. Mary Jane's visitors were still loudly visiting on the other side of the room. Nurses and medical staff were in and out checking on me, and my dear friend, the maintenance guy, was back to drilling right above my head. I looked at my mom and begged her to tell him to get out. Put simply, I was losing it.

Finally, Mary Jane's visitors left, the maintenance guy finished up, and I found myself in a quiet room. The problem was it was anything but quiet in my head. The noise was gone, but I felt as if it was so loud my head could explode. I was in a complete panic and had so much fear of what was happening to me. I lay there crying, trying to calm down.

The experience with the PICC had become much bigger to me than it actually was. The reality was, I was three days in the hospital with things only getting worse. My systems were shutting down, they still did not know what was happening or how to fix it, and I was scared to death. I was 34 years old but still felt like a kid most of the time. I had a husband and a young son. It felt like life was just starting, and I was frightened I might not make it. My heart ached at the thought that I might not make it past this point in time. I might not grow old with my husband. I might not have the privilege of spending my days as a mom to this unbelievable little boy God had blessed me with. To see him grow into a man and watch what he would become. All of that was racing through my mind and breaking my heart. I was thinking about my life to that point and everyone I loved, not knowing if it was all slipping away.

Everything about me was weak; my body, mind, and spirit were worn. I had heard people say that an unknown strength can be found during trying times. I admit that I've learned I am much tougher than I thought. But the strength I found that day did not come from me. God was about to provide all the strength I would need.

I laid there and closed my eyes, and took some deep breaths. I sent up a desperate prayer to God to rescue me. Within a few seconds, I heard a voice coming from the right side of my bed near my head. It was a woman's voice saying, "You're safe, you're so safe." I lifted my head and asked my mom, sitting in the corner of my room, what she had said. "Nothing," she said. I argued with her, saying, "No, I heard you say something." She promised that she had said nothing. I laid my head back down, and as soon as I did, I heard the same voice again, with just one word, "Jesus." I slowly lifted my head to look at my mom and asked her again what she had said. She promised again, "Nothing." As I laid back, I closed my eyes and tried to let it sink in. A wave of peace then came over me that I cannot explain. Everything was finally quiet.

Philippians 4:7 NIV says, *"And the peace of God,
which transcends all understanding, will guard
your hearts and your minds in Christ Jesus."*

That's the only way to explain the peace I felt. Suddenly I knew what had happened. For a few seconds, I experienced Jesus' love—live and in person—as I like to say. I knew without a doubt God was with me. I believe with all that is in me that voice I heard was one of His angels sent to me with a message from Him. In the blink of an eye, I experienced this brief but boundless glimpse of God's grace, hope, and love. It was simply—indescribable.

How great is God's love? I felt it. To my core, I felt it. I can't fully describe it. There are no words to do it justice. It was AMAZING in the truest sense of the word. I had been in His presence in a way I had never experienced. And if that is what it feels like to be in God's presence for a glimpse, I can only imagine what it will feel like when I am fully in His presence one day. When we are home with Him, experiencing the depth of His love for us.

Here is the thing, though, God is always with us. Whether or not we can audibly hear Him, He is there. He is by our side at all times. We are never, ever alone.

God's love is so great that it sustained me over the next two and a half years of my illness. At my weakest, I called out to Him, inviting Him in without hesitation or walls up, surrendering control. I knew God; I believed in Him but never before had I experienced the extent and magnitude of God's love and grace for me as I just had. What I received would carry me through the longest and most painful time of my life. When I wanted to fall asleep and shut the world out, thinking that I could not continue in this battle, I would remember what happened. The moment when God became so real to me, I felt as though I could reach out and touch Him. I knew I was not alone. I knew He would see me through. I knew I was safe in His care.

My life was forever changed that day. I carry it with me. The love and peace that continued to sustain and carry me was a precious gift. Please hear me when I say this same precious gift is here for each one of His children.

FOUR

Trust in the Lord

Trust in the Lord with all your heart, and lean not on your own understanding. Acknowledge Him in all your ways, and He will make your paths straight.

—Proverbs 3: 5-6

As the next days and weeks unfolded, I would never have been able to imagine what was coming. I would go through countless attempts at IVs and PICC lines and would drink contrast and all sorts of nasty liquids for CT scans and other tests. I would go through colonoscopies, ultrasounds, x-rays, barium enemas, and MRIs. I was hooked up for what seemed like forever to catheters, heart monitors, and medications dripping from so many bags at once that it took two IV poles to hold them all. Day after day, I would encounter numerous visits from the same doctors with the same answer; they didn't know what was wrong with me. I never thought after three weeks, I would be transferred to a larger, more specialized hospital by ambulance. I would have a new set of doctors and nurses who didn't know me, misdiagnose me, and send me home. I would return there two weeks later for another long stay and surgery. And return home with a PICC line, IV antibiotics, and drainage tubes, and need home nurse visits for weeks.

What started off as a few days in the hospital turned into a two-and-a-half-year-long illness. At my first stint at the larger hospital, they thought they had determined what happened; they had a good guess anyway. And my numbers made it appear I was getting better. They felt at that point that we may never know for sure what had happened. I still was not feeling well, but after a month in two different hospitals, I was more than ready to go home. I'd had so many antibiotics pumped into me the past several weeks that I was improving, and I looked good enough on paper to go home. I was so homesick; I would not let this chance pass by. Once home, I spent the next couple of weeks trying to regain strength. The hard truth was I was not getting better. The pain was increasing again, and I was worried about where things were headed. I had an appointment scheduled at the two-week mark, and we traveled back not knowing what to expect.

They scheduled me with a gynecologist as they originally thought my problems had started in that area. That doctor's visit will be etched in my mind forever. The doctor wanted to start off by reviewing my history and then an exam. I was certain this was not going to be comfortable. The young nurse in the room offered to let me squeeze her hand while he examined me. I believe she was rethinking that offer soon after he started. I glanced at her at one point to see the shocked look on her face from my tight grip. Next on the list was an ultrasound. This was not the fun ultrasound where a baby is on the screen; it was an internal ultrasound. The doctor came into the room, this time with a colleague who wanted to observe. I should mention here that this was a teaching hospital, so extra people always came along for the ride. There was also the ultrasound tech who was taking her instructions from the doctor. He directed her to move the ultrasound wand in every direction possible. In doing so, he noticed a pattern; when she pushed downward, I experienced more pain.

Remember when I said I would share my story in the most real and raw way possible? This is one of those times. I share it in the hope that it will bring a laugh, but it's also a glimpse into my reality and what was about to become my new normal for two-and-a-half years. The doctor continued to direct the tech's movements, declaring in his thick Indian accent, "Just stay away from her rectum (pause), and she'll be fine!" What?! He said it again and again, each time as if making the discovery for the first time! Like the rest of us had somehow missed it, he had to say it again so as not to leave anyone out. And if that was not enough, he also started yelling, "There is something in her rectum!" I can't begin to recount the number of times those phrases were offered up over the next twenty minutes. His casual use of the word was alarming. As had come to be expected, my tears flowed. While I can laugh at it now, it was horrifically painful at the time. Unfortunately, this particular doctor had no tolerance for my tears and frequently yelled at me, "No cry!" Whenever he thought I was crying too much, he would bark at me again, "No cry!"

He called us into his office to talk after the exam. I was still crying, and he again barked at me, "No, cry." He was softer this time and said, "We are going to find out what is wrong with you." Bless his heart (I can't believe I am saying that now). I think his ordering me not to cry was his way of telling me everything would be okay, but it was hard to see that then.

At this point, he believed we needed to meet with the surgical team and asked us to come back in a couple of days to meet another doctor. The night before our next appointment, I enjoyed my first night out in a long time. I was out with my sister, mom, and grandma. Throughout dinner, I knew something was not right. My head was spinning, and the pain was increasing. By the time I was back home, I was spiking a fever. The next day after meeting with the surgeon, he informed me I would not be going home and admitted me immediately. I cried (again) and begged him to let me go home for the evening. Tyler's 2nd-grade musical that evening, and I told him I was going to be there. The doctor looked at me again, this time quite sternly, and told me under no circumstance would I be going home.

After more testing from the surgical team, they determined I had an internal abscess hiding nicely between some organs, my uterus, and colon, to be exact. They needed to operate. Again, being a teaching hospital, once the surgical teams found out there was an interesting and unusual patient awaiting surgery, each one wanted to pay me a visit. A surgical group in training would walk into my room, introduce themselves, and want to ask a few questions. They would then kindly ask if they could have a quick look. Being the people pleaser I am, I allowed the first team to do so. While I still am a people pleaser to a certain degree, I have learned a lesson or two and can now say no when I need to. The second team arrived only minutes after the first. Dave allowed them to ask their questions, but when it came time to ask if they could take a look, Dave stood up, crossed his arms, and said, "No, you are not touching her." My hero.

After surgery, I spent a couple more weeks at the big hospital before being sent home to recover. My veins had taken more abuse than they could handle, so they decided to send me home with a new PICC line. The night before my discharge, my IV blew. No one was present to start a new line, and they were insistent I could not go overnight without an IV. After 18 attempts (yes, 18), they finally called a NICU nurse to start the IV. For the first time in my life, I felt like a human pin cushion.

The next morning, I received my new PICC line, which I would use to administer IV antibiotics to myself around the clock. I also came home with drainage tubes my dear husband and mom were tasked to tend to (bless them) and a loss of physical strength I can't explain. Gratefully, I also came home rejoicing that I was alive. Why does it take such extreme situations to put life in perspective, to help us understand what is truly important? I'd never been happier to be home with my family and friends who loved us. They delivered meals and prayers, cleaned my house, and decorated it for holidays when I didn't have the wherewithal to do it myself. The support and encouragement we received was a humbling and beautiful gift to receive, and we are forever grateful. Best of all, I came home with Jesus alive in my heart.

While the surgery was successful initially, and I thought I was out of the woods, that did not mark the end of my illness. In June of 2007, it was back, and I was again transported from our local ER by ambulance to the big hospital in the city. Another surgery. Another long hospital stay. In 2008, I was sick three more times, in April, July, and October. Almost like clockwork each time, with another surgery and hospital stay.

Each recurrence of my illness was a punch in the gut. Each time I started to feel sick, I knew what was coming. It was hard to face. I knew the routine, the tests, the IV pokes, the daily heparin shots in my stomach that left me bruised for weeks, the liquid diet, the drainage tubes, and the hospital stays that would keep me away from home. I knew the pain that was barreling toward me. The pain would make me curl up into a ball on the floor because there was no escape. Pain that would make me beg for another dose of medication.

My body was struggling to keep up with the abuse it was taking. All unnecessary functions my body typically took care of shut down so it could take care of the most important tasks at hand. Three months after I first got sick, my hair started falling out. It simply stopped growing as it was not important to my survival. I would stand over my bathroom sink, shake my head, and the sink would be full of hair. In all, I lost about half of my hair. It was unsettling, as it was a visible sign of how sick I was, but it was ok. Creative styling covered up a lot. When those close to me would delicately ask me if I realized I was losing my hair, I could only say, "uh, yes," and grin. Again, I reminded myself of how blessed I was to be here.

While my physical strength was weakened, I lightheartedly told people that my two-and-a-half-year illness was my spiritual boot camp. That could not be truer. I had so many ups and downs I couldn't see straight. In His own way, each time I drifted, Jesus pulled me back closer to Him. I would fall back, rely on my own strength, and eventually fall into despair. I would call out to Him, and He would be there again to rescue me. I would surrender control and remember how my life was so much better in His hands. I was such a difficult student. I could see Him shaking His head at me and thinking, "When is she going to learn?" Luckily, He is the most persistent of teachers. As time went on, I tried more and more to take Him with me everywhere I went.

I have so many memories of my time in the hospital. One that stands out is when someone from patient transport would come to take me from my hospital room to a test. I hated those long rides through the hospital hallways. They were cold and lonely, and I always felt like I was on display. Once they got me to the test site, they put me in a holding room where I would wait. After the test, I would be returned there. Sometimes I would be by myself, sometimes with other patients. The holding room was always dark, quiet, and depressing. It was hard to see everyone lined up waiting for their turn, each facing their own battle. Some of the tests were long and hard. The MRIs were tough for me. I already do not like confined spaces, so lying in a tube for an hour was not my idea of a good time. They gave me earplugs for all the noise the machine made. They offered to cover my eyes, which I definitely let them do so that I would not be tempted to open them during the test and panic. And I was given some medicine to help me relax, which I would not have wanted to go in without.

The most important thing I would take into a test was God. I would lay there, pray and talk to Him the entire time. When I wasn't praying, I would think of a favorite song, "Turn your eyes upon Jesus, Look full in His wonderful face, and the things of this world will grow strangely dim, in the light of his glory and grace." [4] I would lay there and sing it over and over. I don't know

---

[4] Helen H Lemmel. *Turn Your Eyes Upon Jesus*. Glad Songs. British National Sunday School Union, 1922.

what it is about this little song, but it brings me peace. I would not allow myself to drift away from Him for even a second. I knew if I did, I would lose it. If I focused on Him, my trouble would fade away.

In January of 2009, I was sick for the seventh time. We knew it was time to look for answers elsewhere. After many prayers, we ended up at an even larger, more specialized hospital, where they took a new approach. They felt they had the best solution to repair the problem for good. It was a two-part process. My first surgery took place in January. It was relatively quick and easy compared to the other surgeries I had been through, and I eagerly awaited part two. When we went back for our consult on part two, I did not receive the reassurance I was looking for. The doctor talked about it being a complicated surgery and that there was no guarantee it would work. With each prior surgery, the surgeons tried to reach the infection through different routes, leaving me with some open holes internally. The surgeon was going to make sure every little ounce of infection was gone and then repair those openings by doing some tissue grafting. With more hesitation than I liked, we went for it, hoping for the best.

I think the doctor, not purposefully (or maybe so), left out some of the details of the recovery process of this surgery when he prepped me for it. It was probably for the best. I was told I could not move for 72 hours post-op. I must lie on my back with as little movement as possible. So, no moving. No turning on my side. No food or drink. No ice chips. No sponge to wet my parched lips. Nothing. The slightest thing could put my digestive system into action, and it needed to stay asleep so the repair work that had been done would not be disturbed.

For the next 72 hours, I lay there staring at the ceiling, pressing my morphine pump button at every possible interval. The pain was way more than I expected. Morphine was a new drug for me, at least in those doses, and I did not understand what it would do to my mental state. Halfway through day two, I had the panic attack of all panic attacks. I was lying there feeling like I could not breathe anymore and, honest to God, that I was dying. I was flipping out. Luckily my nurse popped her head in the doorway at that very moment to ask if I was doing okay. She took one look at me and knew otherwise. She promised to return quickly, and she did. She returned with some medicine that she promptly put into my IV to calm me. She sat with me and softly talked as I came down from my trip. She assured me that I was okay and that as long as I was on the morphine, she would also make sure I received this medicine as well.

It was inspiring to encounter the people God put in my path to bring me peace or show me that extra dose of love or comfort I needed. They were truly remarkable people who had brought God to work with them. The nurse that rushed to my aide when the morphine overpowered me was one of those people I will never forget. So many nurses and techs prayed with me, fought for me when I was hurting, sat with me, held my hand, and wiped away my tears. There were times when I looked into their eyes, I could sense the presence of Jesus.

One such person was a nurse at the hospital where I had my last surgery. One of my IVs had blown in the middle of the night, and he was having trouble getting a new one started. He said he felt things would go better on his knees and then dropped to the floor and began to pray as he continued to work. As he started the IV, I knew God was there.

I never learned the name of one person who stands out in my mind, perhaps more than any other. He was a patient aide who transported me from post-op to my room after my final surgery. I woke up from that particular surgery extremely nauseated. He was aware of that, and he knew we had a long ride to the room where I was assigned. He had a bucket of warm water and washcloths with him. He was so careful transporting me, trying to take turns gently and bumps smoothly. He went slowly and checked on me every couple of minutes to see how I was. I am not sure how often I got sick on the way to my room. I was lying flat, holding a bucket and aiming for it. Even so, not everything made it into the bucket. He would pull my bed over to the side of the hall, slowly take a washcloth, dunk it in his warm water bucket and then gently clean my face and neck. He did it with such love. He didn't have to do it; it was not part of his job. But he did it because that was the way he approached his work. He was calm and spoke in a soft voice. I honestly can't remember any of his words, but his actions spoke to me. Jesus was apparent in his presence that even though I was feeling my worst, I was in awe of the beauty of his actions.

After what felt like the longest 72 hours of my life, they woke up my digestive system. Once things were working, I was on my way. The doctor felt that everything went as well as it could have surgically, and he was hopeful, but again, it would take time to know if it had worked. I am thrilled to share that it did work. During this time, God put a verse in my mind. I decided to take it as my own.

Proverbs 3:5-6 NIV says, "Trust in the Lord with all your heart, and lean not on your own understanding, but in all your ways acknowledge Him, and He will make your paths straight."

What I felt God was asking me to do during that time was just that – Trust in the Lord with ALL my heart. Every single time I would worry that the surgery did not work, I was to remind myself of this verse. Trust in the Lord with all your heart. Trust in the Lord with all your heart. Trust in the Lord with all your heart. I am not kidding you; some days, I could say that verse a hundred times. I was in spiritual boot camp. And, it was working. I knew God was telling me it was over. But now, He needed me to believe it. I grabbed ahold of that verse and have never let go. I remember the day I checked in with the doctor from home. I was reporting my progress, and he said, "I think it worked; I don't think you need to worry about this anymore." I thought to myself – I know, God already told me.

I'd like to say that my worrying ended immediately, but I am human, and it did not. Over time it lessened and lessened. Every time it crept in, I would say my verse, push the fear away, and hand it to God. I was healed; God had told me it was over. So—it was over. I was taking His word on that. Even all these years later, I will get an odd pain that reminds me of that time, and I quickly go to that verse. It's a promise from God to me. That struggle is over. He conquered it.

FIVE

◆

Never Alone

For I am the Lord your God, who takes hold of your right hand and says to you, do not fear; I will help you.

—Isaiah 41:13

Dave was born two months premature, coming into this world at two pounds, two ounces. He was truly a miracle baby, being that was 50-plus years ago. Because he was premature, he had Retinopathy of Prematurity (ROP). Abnormal blood vessels attached to the retina grew, leading to the retina becoming detached. For Dave, both retinas became detached, and he endured several surgeries as a baby and into his teenage years. He has been completely blind in his right eye his whole life, as they were unsuccessful in reattaching that retina. They were able to install a Scleral Buckle in his left eye, which has kept his retina in place. As a child with vision in only one eye, Dave was always extra cautious. He did not play any sports, but he would be the first to say that would not have been his area of giftedness anyway. He focused on his academics and his friends, enjoying his school experience. His physical limitations never held him back from doing what he wanted.

Here are a few things to know about Dave. Dave loves people. It's where his energy comes from. Being with people fuels him. He was voted most outgoing in his senior year of high school. He will be friends with anyone who will be his friend. He is the eternal optimist. He is always hoping, wanting, and striving for the best, for himself and others. People have described him as wearing rose-colored glasses. He is determined and persistent and will not give up on anything. Those traits have served him well in many ways.

Dave and I were married in 1994. There were no major issues with his vision for the first several years. In 2002, however, the blood vessels in his seeing eye, which had laid fairly dormant, started to wake up. They were growing and multiplying. They were, as the doctors like to describe them, angry. They would bleed and cloud his vision to the point he could not see. After months of unsuccessful attempts with laser treatments, we were told we needed to accept where things were at. We were not ready to give up on his sight and headed to a larger, more specialized clinic to see what else could be done.

We met a doctor there whom we loved instantly, and he performed surgery on Dave a couple of weeks later. I remember those two days in the hospital so vividly. I stayed in a small hospital room with him; the staff had brought in a cot for me to sleep on. It was in an older wing of the hospital, and the tile looked like it was probably laid in the 1950s. His vision going into that surgery was poor. I had to guide him wherever we went. The morning after the surgery, the doctor came to take the bandages off his eye. I felt like I was in a movie. The doctor's only goal that soon after surgery was that Dave would be able to vaguely see him hold up a couple of fingers. To everyone's amazement, when the doctor pulled back the bandages, Dave called the doctor by name and told him it was nice to finally see him.

Dave enjoyed the best vision of his life after that surgery. For five years, he could see things clearer than he ever had. The colors were richer, and the fine details of objects were crisper. He took in the scenery around him as I had never seen anyone do. It never grew old to him. He loves the outdoors, and he would lie in the grass and stare up, focusing on the leaves in the trees, the shapes of the clouds, or the simple blueness of the sky. Perhaps he somehow knew this quality of vision would not last, that he needed to soak it all in while he could. Tyler was a little boy during this time. Dave enjoyed watching Tyler more than ever; he was alive and vibrant. Dave still recalls the time when he could see his son the best. Tyler's little round face, eyes, and ornery smile are etched in his memory to this day. Tyler played little league baseball, and Dave liked nothing more than watching his son during practice or a game. He didn't want to miss anything.

During this time, we enjoyed annual visits to the eye doctor instead of the weekly trips we were accustomed to. Unfortunately, in 2007 the pressure in his eye started to skyrocket. We were back with our favorite doctor. This time it was neovascular glaucoma. Instead of the blood vessels bleeding, they were blocking the natural drainage of the eye and, in turn, causing the pressure in his eye to spike. We were referred to a glaucoma specialist who determined that a tube needed to be placed in Dave's eye that would continually relieve the pressure. The tube was placed and worked well in bringing the pressure into a range we could all live with. Due to the spikes in pressure, there was permanent damage to his optic nerve, and it diminished his overall vision. We were still very grateful for his vision, and Dave adjusted to his new level of sight.

In 2009, only four months following my final surgery, we were back for another surgery. Dave had been fighting glaucoma for several months. The doctors kept adding eye drops to try and control the situation, but they could not keep up with the escalating pressure. The high pressure was taking its toll on his vision. Driving was becoming a struggle. And trying to do a job that had him on the computer most days was nearly impossible. He was working in the automotive industry during this time, which caused a great deal of stress. The industry was tanking, and we waited to see who else had lost their job each Friday, wondering when it would be his turn. In March 2009, his turn came, one month before my last surgery.

The loss of his job surprisingly came with a sense of relief. While the unknown was scary, we also felt more peace than we expected and trusted God to lay the path. In the months leading up to August 2009, the glaucoma was relentless. In August, Dave was declared legally blind. This meant many things, but learning he could no longer drive was the hardest. Dave still had a good amount of functional vision that helped him get around, but he had lost all of his peripheral vision. When the doctor spoke those words, they hung heavy in the air. That loss of independence was something he was not ready for at the age of 38.

The decision was made to put a second tube in Dave's eye to try and gain some control, and on October 8, 2009, that happened. He came out of surgery, and I was escorted back to see him. We had been through this same surgery before, so we knew what to expect, at least we thought so. His eye was covered with a large bandage packed with gauze. The doctor came to see

Dave and was ready to send us to the hotel for the night. Having this eye covered, Dave was completely blind. The doctor told me how I could change the bandage during the night if necessary and walked away. A few seconds later, he was back. He decided to go ahead and change the bandage himself, so I would not need to. As he removed the bandage, there was a lot of blood. We soon knew more was happening, and God had pulled the doctor back to Dave's side.

When he took the bandages off, Dave could not see anything. It was completely black. Dave's eye socket was bulging. The doctor quickly realized that blood vessels behind the eye had hemorrhaged, an occurrence so rare that it had never happened to one of his patients. The hemorrhage was putting pressure on Dave's optic nerve. It would take away all of his vision within minutes if not attended to. Something had to be done immediately. The doctor needed to cut the side of the eyelid open to release the pressure that was building. I was escorted out of the room. With no time to waste or numb the area, the doctor cut the lid open while the nurses held Dave down and in place.

I did not understand what was happening and was alone in the waiting room. All other patients and families were gone. I sat and did the only thing I knew to do, pray. My mind was racing on the possible outcome we might soon face. I tried to keep my focus on praying, asking God to intervene and save his sight. I don't remember how much time passed before I was taken back to see him and learn they were able to save his vision. At this point, he could see light, and that was enough for us.

At the hotel that night (yes, we actually went to a hotel that night instead of staying in the hospital), we got a lot of looks as we made our way to our room. The doctor wanted Dave to leave his eye uncovered so he would recognize if there was any change in his vision. If Dave sensed someone nearby, he would say, "You should have seen the other guy," and laugh. People honestly looked more frightened after hearing that. I don't think either of us slept a wink that night. We were in shock at the "what if." But we were also in awe of God once again rescuing us.

We met with the doctor the next morning and discussed the previous night's events. The doctor, who also had not slept well, explained that, at first, he was comfortable sending us on our way. But as he walked away, he said he felt something pulling him back to the room to take another look at Dave. We could tell that the doctor did not fully grasp what had happened. We quickly jumped in to tell him that we believed it was God who stopped and made him turn around. Dave loves to share this story with people, and how could he not. One of God's miracles was performed just for him. God is certainly good.

I am so grateful that God has built and formed us to be in a relationship with Him at all times. That he did not make us live life alone. I am thankful that He always meets us exactly where we are. That he can turn pain into beauty. That he never intends for us to be self-sufficient in handling our problems. That he longs for us to be dependent on Him. Fully and completely dependent.

On October 19, 2009, we traveled back for a little plastic surgery on Dave's eyelid. Hopefully, that's the only plastic surgery he will ever need. Still, he does enjoy telling people that he has, in fact, had plastic surgery. We spent another night and saw the doctor the next morning before heading home. We were exhausted physically, mentally, and emotionally from the events of the previous weeks, but really from the last three years. We hoped that we may finally have a break.

SIX

◆

Why Not?

For we live by faith, not by sight.

—2 Corinthians 5:7

On October 20, 2009, we arrived home after Dave's follow-up surgery. I went next door to pick up our dog, Max, from the neighbors. My friend met me at the door. She, of course, asked how things went but then said she had something she needed to tell me. They had recently adopted a young lady who was over 18. She had come to the states as a refugee from Uganda. She told me that her younger sister was still in Uganda, and they had also decided to adopt her. She then said another little girl was also in need of a family. She had been praying about this girl named Fiona. Every time she prayed about it, our faces came to her mind.

Believe me, this was the last thing I expected to hear. One of my first thoughts was that I was not even sure where Uganda was. But I would be lying if I didn't say that as soon as she told me this, and when I heard Fiona's name, I also felt God present. I knew what she was telling me was huge. This was not a simple piece of information that I could tuck away and think about once I had recovered from my current state of exhaustion. She said she would email me a picture so we could see her. I went home and told Dave what I had just learned. We went to the computer to see if there was an email, and there it was. I pulled it up and saw the picture of Fiona. We both sat there looking at her. I was silent, but Dave finally said one simple word, "Huh." I'm not sure that is even a word. No words were necessary, however, for me to know what he was thinking. In that one brief reaction, and by the tone in his voice, he was already all in.

Technically it took us a couple of weeks to make the official decision to adopt Fiona. But in our hearts, we knew God had chosen her for us the first time we saw her. She was ours. I was in shock and disbelief, and it took me a couple of weeks to realize this was happening. Two defining moments confirmed what was already in our hearts. We had gone next door to our neighbors to meet the young woman our friends had adopted. We sat and talked to her about Uganda and her life. I'll never forget the feeling I had as we sat with her. I don't recall much of the actual conversation that evening. What I remember was feeling as if the Holy Spirit was using her to speak to us. It was a powerful feeling that neither of us could explain, other than God was speaking to us. We came home that evening, and after some time, we talked to Tyler. Tyler had come next door with us but had sat in another room talking with the other kids. Still, he observed the smile and joy she carried regardless of what had happened to her in her life. We talked to Tyler about Fiona again. We wanted him to be a part of this decision and discuss what this would mean for our family. We finally stopped talking and asked him what he thought we should do. He sat across from us and said six simple words, "You have to go get her." Words spoken by a then ten-year-old embedded in my heart for eternity. The decision, if not final already, was solidified right then and there. It was happening.

That day marked the beginning of a year-and-a-half journey

to bring our daughter home. Remember when I said I knew God was preparing me for something big? I knew this was it. Dave and I had not been able to have another child and had started to gather information on adoption amid the chaos in our lives. We started looking at what we needed to do to start the process. We had outlined in our minds how this would look. We wanted a baby. We wanted to adopt within the US. We had no desire to leave our country's safety and comfortable living. And, I have to admit, I had even thought to myself—God, if you want to work it out so I could get a red-head, that would be super too! (Tyler was red-head, as was I.) Dave and I like to imagine God looking at us and thinking, "Oh, these two kids, have they forgotten who is in control here? Wait until they see what I have in store!"

So here we were with this little girl that He chose for us, plucked right out of the middle of a little village in the heart of Africa. I can see now what I could not see then. He knew exactly what he was doing. He knew the path there would be heart-wrenching and beautiful all at once. He was going with us. He was about to show us an adventure of a lifetime. He would take each step with us and never leave our sides. I met Jesus in the hospital in a whole new way. And, we were about to meet Him again in Africa in a whole new way. He was opening our eyes and our hearts to the world.

If I had not had the experiences of the past three years at that point, I am not sure what my answer to this call from God would have been. I honestly am not sure the courage would have been there. In fact, I'm sure of it. But I was carrying Jesus in my heart in a way I never had. I was carrying a Jesus that fought for me, carried me, comforted me, and gave me the strength and courage again and again to face the day. It was my spiritual boot camp. And, now it was time to take that training to a whole new level. I couldn't turn down the call. It wasn't an option. I was now following Him. He was in charge, and I trusted Him with my life. Before all this, I would be shy about sharing my faith. I am not proud to say that, but it is the truth. However, after what God had brought Dave and I through, we would never again be shy to share our story. I never want to hide the fact that Jesus is alive in me.

As we started telling people what we were doing, we surprised many of our family and friends – they, too, knew this was really big for us. They supported us, though, knowing our decision was made. A few people asked us why we would do this; it seemed like an unnecessary calling. We'd been through a lot and deserved a break. I don't judge those questions. We had some of those same thoughts. But as soon as we would question, we immediately heard Him say—"Why Not? Why not take this leap of faith? Why not see what I have planned?" While we were scared and the unknown was enormous, we chose to answer the call.

SEVEN

The Call

Blessed is she who believes the Lord would fulfill his promises to her.

—Luke 1:45

I kept a blog about our journey during the year and a half we pursued Fiona's adoption. What I am going to share are excerpts of that time. Years later, as I reread some of the passages, I see so much that was left out. In a way, I think the details that were left out were a way to protect me from everything I was experiencing, an attempt to not be too vulnerable. There are things I didn't say, and I want to fill in some of those gaps so that I can remember and never forget meeting Him halfway across the world.

We traveled to Uganda with our friends who were adopting Rachel. We were fortunate enough to walk this journey with them.

My intent in sharing our adoption story is to show how God brought us through it. I went from struggling to control the situation to finally surrendering it to God. I am forever grateful that our story has a happy ending.

After Fiona was home, I wrote about our experience and will start by sharing it here. Oh, my heart—prepare me to let Him lead me always!

The Call

Unknown prayers are being said on our behalf.

He starts laying the path.

The door opens; a picture appears.

A sweet and innocent face, life changes in an instant.

The story begins, a gift awaits.

Eight thousand miles away, His courage carries us.

Walking into a new world, eyes are opened.

We meet, a family complete.

However, the journey has just begun.

Hellos turn into goodbyes, for now.

Feeling lost and alone, all control gone.

Not our battle, but His, we must wait.

Tired and weary, we remember His promise.

At last, the clouds break, joy abounds.

Victory from Him revealed.

She is home, arms left empty now full.

An answered prayer dances before our eyes.

We feel the fullness of His love.

Forever thankful we answered The Call.

Shortly after deciding to adopt Fiona, we got straight to work. We connected with an attorney in Uganda to start learning what we needed to do. We started and completed our home study, got fingerprinted, and background checked. We gathered and organized endless documents and forms to be notarized. We applied for our Passports (I honestly never thought I would have a passport because I was never leaving the country!). We went to our local health department for immunizations for typhoid, yellow fever, and more. We painted the cutest and pinkest room and began to work on the most exhaustive packing list humanly possible. Things were busy, but I was grateful to feel as if we were moving the process along. To be completely transparent, I was a nervous wreck through all of this. I continually had to pinch myself to realize this was happening and not a dream. Everything that was happening around me was so far removed from my comfort zone that I could barely recognize myself.

We received an email from our attorney in Uganda early in the process. The email contained Fiona's birth certificate. As I examined it, I looked at her birth date—May 2. That is also my birthday. While I did not hear God say the words to me, I clearly felt God was telling me, "I have this, do not fear." There was a heaviness that came over me. I felt God placed that in my hands because he already knew how long and difficult this road would be. He wanted to give me something to hold onto when I needed it. And I certainly did. I was grateful to have that promise from Him.

One evening in May 2010, we heard from the attorney in Uganda. He told us that the courts in Uganda were going on recess and encouraged us to prepare to travel soon. In the meantime, he would work on confirming a court date. We went into motion, booking flights and making arrangements. Things were moving quickly, and I could not fathom that I would find myself on the other side of the world within a couple of weeks. There was so much unknown. So much I didn't understand. This leap of faith was only possible through the kind of strength and courage that comes from God.

The scariest thing I did when preparing to go was to leave Tyler. He was so brave for us. He was committed more than any eleven-year-old could be for what was to come. But to look into his face when we were saying goodbye about ripped by heart out. He had seen me leave many times before, not knowing when I would return home from hospital stays. He had to worry more times than a child should about his mom not coming home. He'd been watching his dad for several years now struggle with his eyesight. Things were not easy for him, and I felt responsible for his burden. And, now we were leaving him, for who knows how long, to bring his sister home. I will never forget his tear-stained yet brave face when we said goodbye.

Once on the road, we headed to Chicago for our journey. We were headed to a little village outside of Uganda's capital Kampala, called Gaba. The small, concrete home the girls were staying at was there. They were being taken care of by a woman named Scovia, also known as Mama Scovia. Scovia had, and still has, a home full of kids that need a home for one reason or another. Unfortunately, this is the reality for far too many children in Uganda. However, we knew soon after meeting Mama Scovia that our girls were being loved by a godly woman living out her calling from God. For a woman with little, God provides a way for her to care for children needing a home. She does it with so much grace and joy.

Mama Scovia is a true woman of God. She had been married to a Muslim man for many years; she was one of many wives. At some point, someone shared Jesus with Scovia, and her life was changed. She decided she could no longer live married to a man outside her faith and left with her children. I can only imagine the courage it took for her to leave what she had in order to start a new life on her own. The answer to how and why she did it is so simple when asked about this. She did it to follow Jesus, to live her life doing what God called her to. In her case, it was to take care of children that needed a home. She has never turned a child away. I have asked Mama Scovia if she has ever worried about having all she needed to care for everyone. She quickly answers no. She does not worry because if God has given her a calling, He will also provide. She is a true blessing in this world.

Mama Scovia's son is Livingstone. Livingstone helped Mama Scovia. At this time, Livingstone was single and lived with the older boys in a little house adjacent to Mama Scovia's. Livingstone, more commonly known now as our brother Livingstone, is a man among men. His heart for Christ and all of God's people is a beautiful thing to witness. God has put a calling on Livingstone's heart to care for His flock, and he is fully committed and driven to answer that call daily. Many of Mama Scovia's children have become servants of God in a way I had never seen. With what little they have, they give so generously.

With all of that said, let's start with my first blog post from Uganda.

Bringing Fiona Home – Blog Post, Day 1

We have arrived! We traveled from Brussels to London last night and then onto Uganda this morning. We were filled with many emotions as we traveled from the airport through Kampala and then into Gaba. The conditions are far from what we pictured, but the best part is that we got to spend time with Fiona. She shared many smiles and talked quite a bit. We walked around Gaba with her and saw the sights around here. I am having trouble uploading pictures, so I will try again later. To Tyler - we love you and miss you terribly!

To say I left a few things out is an understatement. I read this now and am in disbelief with the simplicity of the message I shared. I question who that woman was that wrote it. There is so much left out here I don't know where to begin. Maybe I was trying to protect myself, unprepared to lay out what we had already witnessed in a few short hours. Maybe I was protecting my family at home from the reality we had walked into. We had been in Uganda for less than a day when I wrote this. Our driver picked us up from the airport and quickly delivered us to downtown Kampala to meet with our attorney. We had spent two full nights on an airplane, had not showered or changed clothes, and were completely exhausted. I knew I was far from home when I stepped off the airplane. It looked different, it smelled different, and it sounded different. Some of those things are things I now long for, but at that point, it was new and scary. We met our driver and drove for an hour into Kampala. My eyes did not leave the sights passing before us the entire way there. People everywhere, poverty everywhere. Things I had seen on TV looked so different in person. My eyes had been closed my entire life to what most of the world looks like. And now, there I was, close enough to touch it.

After meeting with our attorney, we grabbed some lunch and

headed to Gaba to the guesthouse where we would be staying. We arrived and found our room. As I stood in the bedroom with Dave, reality hit. I burst into tears uncontrollably. I had held it together for the past two and a half days, and now that we were alone, the flood gates of my emotions poured out. The girl that was happy living within the boundaries of her safe world had been catapulted to a place far beyond her comfort zone. We stood in a small bedroom with a bed slightly larger than a twin that we would share. It was covered by a mosquito net. The windows were covered with iron bars and could not be opened due to the bugs. A tall fan stood in the corner. The guesthouse was surrounded by a tall brick wall with barbed wire, a gate, armed guards, and dogs. We were far from home, and I was in a panic about where I now stood, with absolutely no clue what would happen.

We had a couple of hours before Livingstone would be there to meet us and take us to Scovia's house. Having not showered in days, we went to clean up in the bathroom. We got a small amount of water from the faucet, enough to fill a bucket part way, and that is what we had to work with. We cleaned up the best we could and laid down for a while to rest as we waited.

As planned, Livingstone arrived to meet us. We went downstairs to meet him. As I shared, we loved him instantly. Our Ugandan brother. His smile was infectious, and he carried God with him. Shortly after, he took us on a walk to Scovia's house, where we would meet Fiona for the first time. The walk there was short but surreal. We left the guesthouse and walked the red clay streets of the village for the first time, trying to take it all in. We arrived at Mama Scovia's small concrete home and were escorted to a sofa that sat in a small front room. Many kids were running about, and I kept looking at each one, wondering if it was her. Soon, this petite girl walked through the curtain-draped doorway, and Livingstone told us this was our daughter.

In the blog post, I calmly stated, "we met Fiona today." I look at that now and think about all that was left out. I met my daughter that day! The second I saw her, I felt overwhelming love for her. We motioned her to come and see us, and she climbed up on our laps and gave us a big hug. Our first picture with her is one that I love so much. Even though I looked like a hot mess (which I was), I treasure that picture and the little girl sitting on my lap with the biggest smile on her face. After visiting and looking at some of her schoolwork, we went on a village tour with Livingstone. Fiona held her new daddy's hand the whole way, never letting go. I will forever hold that day and that image of the two of them hand in hand. The day the doctor held up our little boy for us to see is embedded in my heart, and so was this. The moment I met each of my children could not have been more different. Yet each created a new love in my heart that will never fade. Both made me a mom.

EIGHT

A New World

Many are the plans in the mind of a man, but it is
the purpose of the LORD that will stand.

—Proverbs 19:21

We were in Uganda for five weeks on our first trip. Within a few days, we realized the court date our attorney had promised us would be much harder to obtain than expected. While this first trip did not end with us bringing Fiona home (spoiler alert), we learned and experienced a brand-new world.

We fell in love with our new family, who we quickly knew would forever be a part of our lives. We worshiped in church like we never had, listened to children praise the Lord with excitement, prayed the "Ugandan way" every evening, and witnessed incredible faith.

While in Uganda, we waited and waited and waited some more. We fired an attorney and hired a new attorney. We had a court date (finally) until we didn't. We shopped in Ugandan markets, ate new foods, and played with bats, bugs, and lizards. We walked along red clay roads with goats, chickens, and long horn cattle. We navigated a foreign land. We had days of peace and days of worry and wonder. We were homesick and scared; we prayed a lot. We learned to depend on God for each step in the process.

I do not believe our first trip was a mistake by any means. God brought us to Uganda. Not for the purpose we thought, but He did indeed bring us there. The following pages contain excerpts of a daily blog I kept. I hope this provides a glimpse into our new world and the little girl who captured our hearts.

Blog Post, Day 2

We are wrapping up our second day in Uganda and are home from walking Fiona and Rachel back to Scovia's house for the night. We spent several hours with them today. Fiona colored for about two hours straight. The girls stayed and had dinner with us. Fiona packed more away in her tummy than I thought possible. I have never seen a child put literally nothing to waste. She shared many smiles and laughs today and is feeling comfortable with us. She repeats many English words right away. She was really interested in the pictures of Tyler and immediately smiled when she saw them. She can say his name too – Tyra – as she calls him.

Last night we were finally able to sleep. It was exciting hearing the sounds outside, everything from roosters crowing, to flutes being played, music, preaching in the streets, and children's voices. Today Livingstone came here for a visit before he brought the girls over, and we spent time hearing from him about what life is like in Uganda. Livingstone's sister, Florence, has been doing the cooking for us along with some other beautiful ladies. They work so hard to prepare the meals. There is work going on in the kitchen from morning until night.

Tomorrow we will go to church. Hopefully, we will hear from our attorney and know about a court date on Monday. The court system is unpredictable, so we ask for prayers that God will move.

Home seems far away, but the people are beautiful, and we are blessed by God for bringing us here. This is a life-changing experience, and we have only been here two days! Much love to you all, and thank you for your prayers.

Day 3

Today was a full day here. We started by going to church. We stopped by Scovia's house to meet her (she has been at her tailor shop the last two days, so we were unable to meet her until now) and then walked with the family to church. We took Fiona and Rachel to their children's church and watched them sing. Livingstone had us sit in on part of a bible study, and then we went to the worship service. Fiona came and found us while we were in church and eventually fell asleep on me.

After church, we came back to the guesthouse and enjoyed lunch together. Livingstone, Florence, and Scovia joined us to discuss the coming week. We prayed the Ugandan way, which is everyone praying out loud at the same time. It was quite an experience.

We took the girls back to Scovia's and then walked through Gaba. While filming our journey through town, we were approached by kids who wanted to see their pictures. One little girl about 12-18 months came up to Dave and wanted to be picked up. He held her, and she played with his scruffy face. The kids love Dave.

Day 4

Each day we fall more in love with these girls. We got to Skype Tyler yesterday with Fiona, so he and grandma and grandpa met Fiona. She was fascinated with the computer and seeing herself on the screen. She smiled, waved, and said goodbye at the end. I brought a little plastic tea set, which was a huge hit. Fiona likes to imitate what we do, so yesterday, I winked at her, and she kept winking back.

Over the past few days, we learned we are sharing this guesthouse with a few unwanted guests. Last night at dinner, a mouse kept running along the side of the wall. Rachelle and I were proud of ourselves for not screaming and running away. Later in the sitting room, Rachelle and I played with the girls, and a bat came in. The girls laughed so hard at us; Fiona even had tears running down her face. Florence said Fiona laughed so hard because she was "not used to seeing mature people react that way." This morning when Dave was bathing, he found a bat in the corner of the tub with him. So glad it was him and not me because he handled it so well. The little bat was actually quite scared, and Florence was able to come and get the trembling bat and take it outside. There are giant flying beetles everywhere, and last night, sitting on the outside balcony, we saw lizards walking around. Hot water is a high commodity here; some days, we have it, and others do not. We can live with all of these things, though, and we'll have stories to share for the rest of our lives.

Fiona came here this morning with her other front tooth gone. They call that space a "divu." They tell the story that a mouse will come tonight and take the tooth, and then she will have pancakes in the morning.

Waiting is the most challenging part here. Hopefully, we will hear about a court date today. We are hitting some roadblocks, but we are choosing to remain faithful to God's plan.

Day 6

Fiona's personality is really bursting out. She brought her teddy bear with her today that we had sent to her. She calls it her baby, and it was dressed in African attire that Scovia made for it. She ate well again today and finished her plate at lunch and dinner (as well as whatever was left on our plates). She does not leave a thing to spare. She played lots of hide and seek, sang a lot, and repeats everything we say. The water was back on, so that was great. And Dave only got chased by one bat today.

Day 7

We started early today when our driver picked us up and headed to the "surgery," which is the doctor's office. Both girls came out dressed in their Sunday best. Fiona had a hanky in her hand; she looked like a little lady. She did well at the doctor until the pokes, one for a TB test and another for an HIV test. She cried hard when she got poked and wouldn't look at us for some time.

This little girl has undoubtedly stolen our hearts, reminding us in many ways of Tyler. They should get along great. Things are moving slower than I would like, but I am confident this little girl will be ours; she already is. She weighed in at 35 pounds and about 41 inches tall today. She is probably a couple of pounds heavier than she was a week ago with all she has eaten!

Still homesick. This will all be worth it when we bring our daughter home. Please pray that we will not fear, but open our hearts to trust in Him.

Day 9

As our driver told us the other day – TIA. We asked what this meant, and he said, "This is Africa." That phrase keeps coming to mind when things don't go as we would like. We are going on 36 hours of no running water. The girls helping us at the house are filling up jugs of water to bring upstairs so we can flush the toilet and take small baths. The simple things we take for granted. Water and power outages are common here as they shut off certain areas for a while to ensure everyone has enough. The water is usually cold, which is fine. We just want running water.

Mark, Dave, and Livingstone went into Kampala today with the girls to get their TB test results read. A little daddy/daughter outing. It was better than five of us crammed into the back of a Camry.

Fiona was sweet as always today. She and Rachel talked and sang, which is always a joy. When we get frustrated with this process, we look at them and know why we are here. Today they were singing, "All the children of the world." Fiona wore her famous teal skirt today, which seems to be her favorite. It has sparkles and flowers all over it.

We ended this day with a great prayer with Florence and Livingstone. We love to listen to them pray. We also end this day with no electricity, which equals no fan tonight. It is hot. Florence and Livingstone said we are becoming true Ugandans.

Day 10 & 11

We are still here. We didn't get to post yesterday as we were still without electricity, and all electronics ran out of juice. Good news for today - electricity came back on. We were so happy to have it after more than two days without. Water also came back on last night - cold - but we do not care.

Today we went to the "surgery" for the girl's last medical exam. Then we went to a mall in Kampala to an internet cafe since we needed to check and send emails. The girls got to ride in an elevator for the first time too. Came back here for a fun afternoon of playing. Fiona and Rachael got their fingers and toes painted. Fiona had fun showing them off as she danced and looked at her pretty nails.

The registrar is back in court, and we are still waiting for word. Our big prayer request for tonight is that we will hear some concrete news tomorrow on a court date.

Day 12

Today started with breakfast and a long walk to the local "grocery store," which consisted of two isles. We were able to do laundry after many days of not being able to. The washing machine at our guest house takes about 3 hours to run through the complete cycle. Then we hang our clothes out to dry on the balcony with clothes pins. Funny how the simple things in life make us happy right now, water, electricity, and doing laundry.

Tyler had his 5th-grade graduation today at school, and we were sad to not be there to celebrate with him.

We had carry-out Uganda pizza tonight from town. It was different than the pizza from home, but it was good and a nice change of pace. Florence, Teddy, and Jen have been feeding us very well. They serve several items at each meal, and boy, do they love their carbs here. On average, there are at least three carbs served at each meal. Rice, potatoes of many varieties - sweet potatoes, roasted potatoes, mashed potatoes, French fries (which they call chips), toasted bread, and chapattis - which is like a fried tortilla. We love it all. They also serve lots of pineapples, avocado, beef stew, chicken stew, pea soup, and lots of beans.

Day 13

We feel we are at a crossroads because we do not know how much longer to wait for a court date with us staying in-country. One option is for us to come home and wait and then travel back. This is not what we want, and the thought of leaving is hard to imagine, even for a little while. At the same time, we cannot see God's plan in front of us as to when this will happen.

We prayed with Scovia, Florence, Livingstone, and Teddy. Scovia said that when she heard we wanted to pray tonight, the Lord directed her to Jeremiah 29:11-14. "For I know the plans I have for you, declares the Lord. Plans to prosper you and not to harm you, plans to give you hope and a future. Then you will call upon me and come and pray to me, and I will listen to you. You will seek me and find me when you seek me with all your heart. I will be found by you, declares the Lord, and will bring you back from captivity. I will gather you from all the nations and places where I have banished you, declares the Lord, and will bring you back to the place from which I carried you into exile."

Day 15

We headed out to Kampala for the day. We took matatus, which are bus/taxi-like vehicles. They stop often, drop people off and pick people up, so there is a lot of moving around in the vehicle at every stop.

We also went to the local mall. There are two right next to each other, and Livingstone tells us they are the only malls in Uganda and that people from all over come to shop there. We had some lunch and then hit a bookstore. We hired a taxi to bring us home, which was a much quicker route. I sat in front for the first time, and wow, was that an experience. I have never seen driving like this in my life. It is insane. There are people everywhere, bikes, motorcycles, matatus, cars, all driving on the wrong side of the road, and it looks like one big mess. I prefer sitting in the back.

One of the saddest things I have seen here happened today. While walking to the mall, we saw a one-year-old, I would guess, sitting on the sidewalk all by herself. Livingstone said parents will drop their kids places like that and think maybe someone will pick them up during the day. She looked so sad. Rachelle gave her some water to drink. Several kids were begging along the road, and they would run out into the traffic when cars were stopped. One little boy about two years old was attempting to come over to our car in traffic. He was waving, and I waved back, and he was going to cross into traffic to come to our car. Luckily, he did not cross the road. What a dangerous life these kids are living. I am saddened by the desperation I see.

A couple of days ago, Livingstone took us on a walk to Munyonyo, an upscale side of this area. He took us to the Speke Resort to look at the lake. It was beautiful. What a walk, though. It took us about an hour and a half to get there. We opted for a matatu for part of the way back. I got my first African sunburn. We all got a little toasted that day. My legs are also getting covered in mosquito bites. It seems they prefer me to the others here. I will be careful not to miss a dose of my malaria medicine.

I wish I could adequately describe the sights I am seeing. The drive to Kampala and back is like nothing I have ever seen. I thought I had an image of what Africa would look like, but I was way off. And, I know there is much more than what I am seeing.

I am homesick and missing family, friends, and home. Some days are better, and on others, I feel it more. The love we have for these girls keeps us moving forward. A friend told me before I left that it may seem like a long time I am gone, but in the end, it will only be a flash of time in my life. So, we will move forward and enjoy these girls and the time we have here and the company of the beautiful people God has put in our lives here.

These girls have been through so much in their young lives. Scovia has taken such good care of them and raised them so well. They are so polite and obedient. We think the rest of our kids could use a week with Mama Scovia.

Day 16

Today was a quiet, lazy day. After lunch, Livingstone stopped by. Dave had been looking for a Ugandan flag. Livingstone found one and brought it to us. Then we were off to Mama Scovia's tailor shop to pick out some fabric. Dave and Tyler are each getting a nice shirt, Fiona is getting a dress, and I am getting a shirt and skirt. All in the same fabric - won't we be cute.

We had dinner, and the girls finished taking baths and brushing their teeth, so they are off to bed soon. We will go to church tomorrow, and then we are hoping to teach Florence how to make peanut butter cookies.

Day 17

Happy Sunday! Our day started with church. Dave and I decided to sit in on kid's church today. We listened to the kids sing many songs and listen to a bible story. Then, we went to a Sunday school class with Fiona. Church was still in progress, so we finished listening to the sermon there.

We have not slept well the last couple of nights. These people know how to party here all night, and I mean all night. And Sunday is their favorite night to party.

Day 19

We have to decide what our plan is. If we do not have a hearing this week or next, we may need to go home and come back when we have a hearing date. We are trying to trust in God's plan for us here. I am having a hard time thinking that may mean leaving Fiona.

Rachael, Fiona, and their friend Trust, all went into the bathroom and locked the door (not sure why). It's an old house with key locks, and they could not get it open. It was mass hysteria when they discovered they could not get out. Florence had to come upstairs and speak to them in Luganda so they could understand what we were telling them to do to get out.

Day 20

Met with a new attorney today and thinking of having her represent us. Our hearts are split between home and here. The phrase "there is no place like home" is taking on a deeper meaning for us as we realize how unbelievably blessed we are to have you all in our lives and the comfort that home brings. And then we have this little girl here who we have fallen in love with and have to bring home. We talked about it again today, how only God could have plucked this little girl out of the middle of Africa for us. She was meant to be ours.

Day 21

Our new attorney is filing papers with the court tomorrow on our change in legal representation and to have our file transferred. We will most likely hear on Monday about our hopeful June 14 hearing.

Day 22

Today we spent most of our time in Kampala, where we visited the craft market. Then we walked to the mall and had lunch. Livingstone tried his first cheeseburger. He loved it. The downtown area was so busy today, and getting a matatu back to the taxi park was nearly impossible. So, we decided to walk. The number of people here is amazing. We were weaving in and out of traffic, and no sidewalk was free from holes and uneven pavement, so maneuvering myself with Dave through all of this was a little stressful. Mark equates it to the old video game Frogger. It's a pretty good description of what it is like in Kampala.

We came back and had dinner, and then Livingstone and Florence helped us sit down with the girls and explain what is happening over the next few weeks. They understand some, but the language barrier is still there. They are going to start school again on Monday. They go to school year-round here, three months at a time, and then take a month off. We can take the girls to and from school each day and do homework with them.

Tomorrow we are going to the market with Florence to get some items we need to make a Chinese meal. We are making egg rolls and chicken fried rice. They enjoy trying new foods, and seeing their reactions to them is fun. We are falling more in love with our extended family here. Livingstone, Florence, and Teddy are some of the most wonderful, giving people.

We are pleased with our progress this week in finding new representation and for God giving us that direction.

Day 24

The waiting is hard here, but this morning church was just what I needed, and each day God gives us here is really a gift. We've learned so much that we will always have with us.

Then we were off to buy school supplies in the market. The list of items is much different. There are the things you would expect like pencils and paper. Other required items include toilet paper, shoe polish, a shoe brush, an inside broom, an outside broom (a bunch of sticks tied together), and socks to match their uniforms. The girls also got their first book bags, which were a big hit. They are both really excited about getting back to school. They polished their school shoes tonight, and Teddy is pressing their uniforms. They are excited to bring us to school in the morning to see it and meet their teachers.

Tomorrow we will hopefully meet with our attorney and receive a court date. Please be in prayer about this for us. We had fun talking to Livingstone, Florence, and Teddy tonight. Livingstone asked us if a man brings livestock (goats, cows) to the bride's family before marrying. We said no; the bride's family usually pays for everything in America, and they couldn't believe it.

Day 25

Today the girls started school and were excited to be doing so. They got up early and were ready on time. We walked them to school, paid their fees, and then took them to their classrooms.

I called our attorney, and we have arranged to meet tomorrow morning. I asked if she was working on a court date, and she said she was still in her workshop today and would do that tomorrow. Maybe it is the language barrier, but things always seem confusing and happen a day later than expected.

Our return airline tickets are for this coming Saturday, which we will need to be changing in the next couple of days. We need to get some direction tomorrow on a court date so we can re-book our tickets.

We are praying that we will be able to see God's plan here for us. We are sure that God has put us into a relationship with the Lule family, which will continue long after we leave.

Day 26

Today was a good day and one that we have been waiting and praying for. We have a court date on June 14.

We met with our attorney this morning and feel comfortable with her. This judge typically gives rulings a few weeks after the initial hearing, so it looks like we will be flying home for a while we wait.

A lot still has to happen, but we feel good about the progress. Thanks for all the prayers, and please keep them coming for Monday.

Day 28

Tomorrow is Dave's birthday - so we will have everyone over to dinner to celebrate. We are going to do our Mexican meal again at his request.

We are booked on a flight to head out Thursday night and will arrive in Chicago Friday afternoon. We should have a good idea of when we can return after our hearing on Monday.

Day 30

At about 2:00 a.m. last night, we were asleep. Suddenly, I woke up feeling something crawling on my arm. I opened my eyes to see something black crawling inside the mosquito net. I quickly woke Dave up, and we looked to see what it was and could not find anything. Upon further inspection, we found a bat in the sheets at the bottom of our bed. The bat then went under the bed. We evaluated the situation for some time and did not know how to get it out of the bedroom. So, there we were, waking up Teddy to come to rescue us from the bat. She showed no fear and, after a few minutes, had it in a bag. Going back to sleep was a challenge, I must say.

Today we prepared dinner for everyone, a Mexican fiesta for Dave's birthday. We had homemade salsa, guacamole, chips, potatoes, eggs with Mexican sausage, chapattis, and fried chicken. I made the chapatti today and am looking forward to making it when we get home.

Florence got a cake for Dave's birthday. A cake for someone's birthday is a big deal here in Uganda. It is a luxury to have one. Livingstone made homemade signs wishing Dave a Happy Birthday, and they sang to him several times. Scovia came for dinner too and stood up and sang herself while dancing. Livingstone also gave Dave a birthday gift, some wooden sandals he carved himself. They have all called Dave the "baby" for the last two days, which is what they call the birthday boy or girl. So, he's been, Baby Dave.

Day 31

Tomorrow is the big day. We are going to court. Church was fabulous. It was a wonderful time of worship, and the theme for the day was surrendering it all to God. Perfect. We will post news as soon as we have it tomorrow.

Day 32

What a day this has been. On our way to our attorney's office, we received a call that our judge told her clerk to send our files back to the registrar to be reassigned. She was on her way to the courthouse to see what she could do. She said the judge told her that she would not hear any new cases - even though we had a court hearing scheduled. We went with her to the courthouse to meet with the registrar in person. The registrar first said that it would be the end of August before we could be seen and then asked if we were willing to take a gamble. One of his clerks said that another judge had said he could help and see some cases on Thursday of this week. Sarah was told to come back on Wednesday to confirm this, and if it is a go, we will see him on Thursday morning. We fly out late Thursday night. Nothing like the 11th hour. The registrar said if this does not work, we need to plan for the end of August.

So, that is where things stand right now. Fiona and Rachel did great today; it was a lot of waiting. We ate lunch at a Ugandan buffet-type restaurant. Dave did not realize it until after he ate it, but the meat he had was goat. He did not like it as it had lots of gristle and bones.

God is in control here. Sarah kept saying, "Sometimes our plan is not God's plan." She is right; we are glad to have her as our attorney. She told us that, as all this was happening, she was praying for God to help her. We continue to trust in His plan.

Day 33

Today the girls went to school, and we toured places to stay here with Florence and Jennifer when we return. We have a couple of good options for where to stay next time. The guesthouse here has been okay, but the wildlife inside has been too much for us to return. Spiders, GIANT flying cockroaches, bats, beetles, lizards, mosquitoes, ants, rats, and mice.

Day 34

Today did not bring the news that we wanted. Sarah went to the courthouse and was told that the judge that would hopefully see us tomorrow would be out sick. She is going back in the morning to confirm a court date for a few weeks out. While this is not what we wanted to hear, and it was disappointing, we keep reminding ourselves that we are on God's timetable here, not our own.

A fellow adoptive mom shared a fitting verse today. Habakkuk 2:3 "But these things I plan won't happen right away. Slowly, steadily, surely, the time will come when the vision will be fulfilled. If it seems slow, do not despair, for these things will surely come to pass. Just be patient. They will not be overdue a single day."

I am going to leave it at that tonight. We have received so many blessings and have grown so much. Tomorrow will be hard, but God will provide what is yet to come.

NINE

Back in Africa

My help comes from the Lord, the maker of
Heaven and Earth.

—Psalm 121:2

We made it through the rest of the summer, and in August, we finally learned that we had a court date in September. We were happy to be home and anxious to be back in Uganda at the same time. We decided that Dave would stay home with Tyler for this trip and that Rachelle and I would travel together for court. And, we were off! Following are more excepts from my daily blog.

September 15

Wow, I can't believe we are back in Africa. Our flights were pretty uneventful getting here. Chicago to Amsterdam was an overnight flight. It was a full flight and noisy, so little sleep was had. We had a four-hour layover in Amsterdam, so we decided to grab a quick breakfast sandwich. I saw a sign for "comfort seating" and thought maybe we should go check it out. There was an area full of these reclining chairs, and Rachelle and I quickly found the last two available and decided to take a rest. Three hours later, I woke and looked at my watch, which did not have the local time, so I thought, hmm, I better go see what time it was. It was 10:30, and our plane was leaving at 11:00. I quickly woke Rachelle, and we got to our gate. As we went through final security, the gentleman said, "you are the last ones today." And we were indeed the last people to get on the plane. As we were lying in those lounge chairs, I kept hearing a lady on the intercom saying, "passenger so-and-so, your flight is about to leave. If you do not check in immediately, your luggage will be removed from the plane." The next announcement would have been for us in those chairs after a few more minutes. I told Rachelle they should have warning signs that once you sit in these chairs, you will immediately fall asleep. There were probably 50 chairs, and someone was asleep on every one of them.

The girls were at school this morning, so we surprised them at lunchtime to pick them up. Fiona came to me immediately with a big hug, but eye contact and smiles took a while. Within a couple of hours, she acted more like herself, singing and smiling. Although they knew we were coming back, I am sure for a five-year-old, it is hard to understand, and three months had to seem like forever wondering if we would indeed be back. She spent the afternoon coloring and playing with a doll I brought her, whose hair (by the way) has already been braided. At the end of the day, she is sleeping beside me, and I am so happy to be back with her. In less than two days, we will be in court and are praying to hear the judge say good things.

As I wrote tonight, the power went out. We are definitely back in Africa! The sights and smells are familiar this time, but still amazing to take it all in again. It is the rainy season, so the temps are a bit milder. I actually used a blanket last night.

September 16

Day two in Africa started early as Fiona and Rachel had a field trip at school they were going on. Last night Fiona slept pretty well. She woke up several times in the night and would put her little hand on my arm and say, "Mom?" I would say, "Yes, I am still here," and she would go back to sleep. At 4:30, she was ready to play, so she got out of bed to get her new doll and then returned to bed asking for stickers. I told her it was still nighttime and to go back to sleep. She did, thank goodness!

Tomorrow is the day we have been waiting on for months— court. How do I feel on the eve of our court date? Surprisingly peaceful. This trip feels so different from our last one. I think God's got this all worked out.

September 17 - COURT

Today was the day we have been waiting for; we went to court! There were 8 cases being heard, and we were all in one courtroom. We felt good about how things went, and we are to return at 9:00 for the ruling next Friday. After that, we grabbed lunch and got the girls' passports and visa pictures at the mall. After returning to the hotel, Livingstone suggested we bring the bags/care packages to all the kids at Mama Scovia's house that were wonderfully put together by so many. They were a HUGE hit.

To say the least, we are physically and mentally exhausted this evening. I don't think there is such a thing as a "short" day in Africa. Every day is full, and we are so tired at the end of each one. We are grateful to have been in court and ask for your prayers this next week as we await a ruling.

September 18

Today we went to Scovia's house to help prepare for a party they are throwing tomorrow for one of her daughters that graduated from university in biblical studies. The party will take place at church following morning services. They expect about 400 people, so there is a lot of food to prepare. Rachelle and I got to peel plantains, Irish potatoes, and yams. When we arrived, women were sitting in a circle working. The pile of peelings in front of them was incredible. We took lots of pictures to prove all of our hard work. The family and their helpers will be back at Scovia's at 1:00 a.m. to start cooking all the food. It is quite the process to prepare. It was a unique experience to share this time with the African women. They laughed a few times when we didn't quite get the hang of things and would stop to show us how to do it better.

We headed to the hotel for the evening and some dinner. In the lobby, we talked to the hotel manager and asked about the helicopters that were overhead all day. He said a big event was happening at Munyonyo, a resort we visited the last time we were here. The main event this afternoon? Goat racing. He couldn't believe we had never heard of such a thing. We told him that we race horses in America; he was also surprised by that.

We like the hotel a lot, but last night a hall door was left open after it got dark, and a couple of our furry flying friends found their way to Rachelle's room. On my way to her room, I found one and went downstairs to get the staff to help us. They, too, laughed at our fear of bats. Once we all had called it a night, Rachelle nervously came knocking on my door. While lying in bed, a bat jumped on her chest. I called downstairs, and they sent some staff up to help. It flew out of the room and towards her, and she screamed loud enough to wake the whole house. The bat was caught by a brave young man, and we all found ourselves back to bed, a little more nervous about our surroundings and noises, but we got some sleep.

Tomorrow, we have church followed by the party. I love church here; it always does me good, lifts my spirits, and confirms His plan for us. The worship is simply amazing and spirit-filled.

I got to Skype with Dave and Tyler, and it did me a lot of good to see and talk to them. Fiona talked with them a little bit too. Happy Sunday, and be blessed.

September 19

Our day started off great with church. I've said it before, but these people know how to do church. The pastor talked about how we are all charged with being witnesses of God no matter how shy or incapable we think we may be. The church runs a baby home called Loving Hearts, and during service, they brought their 19 babies in to dedicate them. A couple of families from the US are also in the process of adopting from this home. Scovia's sister Christine works there, and we will schedule a visit. There was also a band from the US here for the Love Kampala festival that is coming up this weekend. They performed and were fabulous.

We also had the graduation party for Agnes. It became an all-day event. *They served lunch at the house following church. The party at church was to start at 2:00 but did not actually start until after 5:00. That is what you call Ugandan time. There is no such thing as a set schedule. Many folks got up to say a few words to Agnes, and many sang. All in Luganda, so we didn't understand much of it. After a couple of hours of that, they served dinner. Usually, when we are at Mama Scovia's, they will give us silverware, although they do not use any. At the dinner, however, there was no silverware. So, Rachelle and I ate our first dinner like any other Ugandan, and that was with our fingers. One of the photographers got a great picture of us. Everyone was so kind and made us feel welcome. It was already dark, and we did not bring flashlights, so Livingstone walked us back to the hotel in the dark. Ugandans are used to seeing in the dark, so it is not hard for them, but we had to take each step carefully. Much like God takes us just one step at a time, without seeing the whole path.*

September 20

Today the girls were introduced to Barbies and Princesses, which were a huge hit. They LOVED them. They did their hair, changed their clothes, and carried them on their backs like African women carry their babies.

Tomorrow we will go to Cassia Lodge for a day of swimming. Rachel and Fiona have never been swimming. We are not sure if they will be afraid or love it.

We visited with the Canadian nurses staying at the hotel. Today they went to the local hospital for a visit. They said they will never again complain about their nurse-to-patient ratio. The labor and delivery unit had over 50 women – in labor! Three nurses were staffed to handle this load. Livingstone and Florence's grandfather has been in the hospital, and Florence has been there daily taking care of him. This makes sense now because if you do not have a loved one there to care for you, you may not get any of the care you need.

September 23 - Trust in the Lord with all your heart.

Here we are on the eve of our ruling. It is hard to believe what we have waited for is now here. It's hard to describe how I feel, but I know God is in control. In Africa, so much of what happens is not in our control. We've learned to lean on Him and trust that He will see this through. In this battle, we want and need God to fight for us because He is the only One that can make this happen. Tomorrow I will do my best to sit back and let God work, knowing He is fighting for us. I want it to be a testament to Him.

This verse has gotten me through many worrisome times, "Trust in the Lord with all your heart." After my last surgery, I repeated this verse to myself constantly, not allowing myself to worry about getting sick again. I was trusting that God had taken care of my problem for good. I think I will use this same verse tomorrow. Lots of love to you all. Court is at 9:00 a.m.

September 24 - Adoption Granted!

I have been waiting for months to be able to write this post and share that the judge granted us adoption today of Fiona! We are officially her parents! I have cried a few tears throughout this process (hard to imagine, I know), but today I cried tears of joy. How often in life do we get to cry real tears of joy? How blessed we are! God is good!

September 26

Today we went to visit a village called Katogo. It is right next to Gaba. This is an area they call a slum. The houses are small, a few feet by a few feet, and are made from sticks and mud. When it rains, homes can be easily washed away. This is the poorest area I have seen since being here. The children still smile, but there is a stark difference in the atmosphere compared to Gaba, where there is a lot of activity, music, shops, and the market area. In Katogo it was quiet and solemn. It is hard to see this kind of poverty. They have a couple of wells that missionaries have come in and drilled to get clean water. There is little money for food or basic needs, and none of the children can go to school. Another humbling experience.

When dinner was ready, Rachelle was not feeling well, so the girls and I went to the little dining room to have dinner. I had asked the staff what the dinner options would be and had ordered fish and chips. Sounded good, I thought. When dinner was served, two large fish were cooked whole, with heads, tails, fins, and eyeballs. This will be a dinner I will remember, as Fiona and Rachel were thrilled with what they saw. Scovia has had this at home occasionally, and the girls love it prepared this way. The fish was cut into three parts, the head, middle, and tail. Racheal picked the head, which is what Fiona also chose. They both started with a head. I watched as they picked every last piece of meat off the bones, pried the mouth apart to get to it all, and ate the eyeballs, which is quite a treat here as it brings good luck to the person who eats it.

We head back to Kampala tomorrow to get our written ruling and work on passports and visas. It is possible we could come home this next weekend.

September 27 - We Have Our Written Ruling

Today we spent all day in Kampala trying to get things going on passports and visas. I am happy to say that all passport documents have been turned in to the passport office, and we have our WRITTEN AND SIGNED RULING from the judge. It was exciting to see it in writing with the judge's signature and official court seal. We hurried into Kampala and spent most of our day waiting, but that was fine.

We had hoped to make it to the Embassy today. But about an hour before it closed, there was a huge downpour, and we got stuck in traffic because of flooded intersections. Seeing how flooded the roads got in such a short time was unbelievable. People were walking in knee-deep water.

We ended our day at Quality Hill, a little coffee shop that is a favorite destination. Lattes, tea, hot chocolate, and pastries hit the spot. I can't end a post without thanking you all for your prayers. I feel like a broken record sometimes, but I want you all to know how grateful we are for them.

September 28 - Each Day a Step Further

Today we got up bright and early to make it to the US Embassy when they opened. We were told that, most likely, our appointment would not be until Monday. I guess He will determine how much longer we are here. We told the clerk that we had scheduled flights next Thursday, and she said even with appointments early next week, we should have our visas in time to travel. I can at least say I will be home next week, which sounds pretty good.

We are definitely in a waiting mode right now. Please keep the final stages of this in your prayers. Many families here are working through the same process, all wanting to get home. This all requires a great deal of patience and faith, so please keep them in your prayers as well.

September 29 - Waiting

We continue to wait on an appointment time from the Embassy. We hoped to get it sometime today, but now we hope for tomorrow. Everything involves waiting here, which we are getting used to, but we still are anxious and ready to get this scheduled.

Tonight, I asked Fiona if she knew what her middle name would be when she got to America. I told her it would be Grace, and she beamed.

September 30 - If God Is for Us, Who Can Be Against Us

This is a song we sang at church on Sunday. I have thought about it a lot this week. God is in control of all that is going on here, and if He is for us, which He is, then who can be against us? It is hard to explain how things are here sometimes. It is a different world, and the systems in place make it extra challenging to accomplish what we need.

Today, we spent our day waiting. We were to stop by the facility that did Fiona's medical exam last time we were here, but the doctor that did her exam is no longer there. So, I had to wait to see another doctor to have him certify a new copy. Three hours later, I finally walked out with it. We will go to the Embassy in the morning to ensure it is sufficient to meet the requirements.

The rest of the day was spent at the passport office. Our passport was supposed to be done today, but we had to get one more signature to complete it for processing. This signature took hours to obtain, getting shuffled from one person to another. We finally got it, though. We are to go back tomorrow at 4:00 to pick it up.

It is essential that we have both of these things resolved tomorrow so we can have an Embassy appointment next week. We felt like the devil was trying to come in and complicate these last few details. I hate to admit it, but I spent most of the day today worrying. I reminded myself that the only thing worrying does is take strength out of you, which it definitely did. I have to turn these things over to God.

I ask for prayers tonight that God will go before us tomorrow and make our path straight. At the end of the day, I have my sweet girl sleeping beside me.

October 1 - Praise God for He is Good and Faithful

Today was another long day in Kampala, but a successful one. We arrived at the Embassy shortly after they opened to check on the medical report. We have confirmed Visa appointments on Monday. This will give us plenty of time to have the visas processed and fly home on schedule.

After the Embassy, we decided to hit the clothing market. It was claustrophobic, people everywhere, pushing our way through crowds - and after a few minutes, I had to get out. We quickly found some tennis shoes for the girls to wear home and a couple of outfits and found our way to the craft market, where we picked up a few items.

We headed to the passport office and had success there. We left with both passports in hand, which leaves us one step away from coming home, and that is our Visa appointment on Monday. They checked through our paperwork this morning to ensure everything was there, so we should be good to go. Scovia will join us as our witness to testify that the girls are orphans. God continues to teach us here. I prayed last night and this morning for God to go before us at each of our destinations today and that He would work through each person to accomplish what we needed. My worry yesterday consumed me, but I had to let go and let God work for us. And He did, of course.

Someone commented on the Ugandan Adoption page yesterday: "When will I let my worry go?" I so completely understand this comment. It is hard to go through this without nerves and emotions getting in the way. These are our kids; we would do anything for them. We depend on others to provide us with what we need. God is bigger than anyone and can work through the toughest people and situations. We have to continually seek His help and ask for His peace. God knows we will not always be as strong as we want or need to be. Luckily, we don't have to be because we have Him.

When Mama Scovia has all the kids around her, she will say, "God is good," and the kids will respond, "All the time." And then she'll say, "All the time," and the kids will respond, "God is good."

October 2 - The Countdown Is On

Five more days, and we will be headed home. The girls had Saturday afternoon church activities, but Fiona needed a nap, so she stayed here while Rachel went. I have not left the hotel all day. That also means I have not sweated today, which may be a first.

Monday is the big day. Our visa appointments are at 2:00 p.m. It feels strange because we have run out of things to do. The waiting is still hard, but we will enjoy our last few days in Uganda.

The hotel owner's daughter is having her "introduction" at the hotel tomorrow. They are preparing for 400 people to attend. It is custom to have an "introduction" ceremony before the wedding. This is where the bride and groom's families are formally introduced to each other. The groom presents his gifts to the bride's family, which many times involves gifts of cows and livestock. Preparations have been going on all day here (which has included the killing of more chickens than I can count, as this was my background noise all day). It will probably be noisy as they cook all night. The owner's wife has invited us to come and join them. We won't fit in as everyone will be dressed in their finest African dresses, but we stand out wherever we go, so nothing new.

October 3 - Visa Appointment Tomorrow!

The "introduction" ceremony for the owner's daughter was today. When we left for church at 10:15, many folks were already arriving. It is now 9:00 p.m., and the party is in full motion. The music is so loud that sleep will not be an option. I have no idea when that will be. No noise ordinances here. Many party guests are staying at the hotel, so there is lots of commotion in the hallway. I think we are the only non-party people staying at the hotel.

When we returned from church at 1:30 were told lunch would soon be served and to go ahead and find seats. We did and three hours later had "lunch." African timing is so different than what we are used to in America. Fiona fell asleep on me, and we finally returned to the room. Soon after, lunch was served, so we went back down. Seeing all the traditions associated with the ceremony is fascinating, but we can't understand a word being said. There were hours of speeches and presentations of gifts from the groom's family to the brides. Now they are dancing and partying until the wee hours of the night.

Tomorrow is the big day - our visa appointment is at 2:00 p.m. This will include lots of paperwork to be reviewed and an orphan investigation.

Please keep prayers coming. This is the final step to us getting home. I feel good about it and know God will be there with us. My family is a little excited to finally meet this little girl in person after all these months. So happy that we will soon be home and can start life with our new addition. Fiona is anxious to see Daddy again and finally meet her big brother. Four more days!

TEN

Hoping, Waiting and Praying

When you pass through the waters, I will be
with you.

—Isaiah 43:2

October 4 - Visa Appointment Complete

We had our Visa appointments today. A lot of the time was spent reviewing forms and getting signatures to complete the file. Scovia was then called in and explained how she found Rachel and Fiona, took them in and cared for them. An orphan investigator goes out in the field to collect information and write a report. This has been done, but he still needs to type it and turn it in. They have tentatively set up for us to come back on Wednesday to pick up the visas unless they run into any problems before that or it's not ready.

Tonight, I ask for prayers for the Embassy employees working on our cases. I pray that God will go before us and work in every situation and person. This process is not easy. I can't do this alone. I have to invite God along through each step. God has moved many mountains for us; this is just one more for Him to move. He continues to ask me to trust in Him with all my heart. I believe He has a story for us to tell, a story of turning what seems like an impossible situation over to Him. He's been working on this with me for a few years now - I guess I am a tough student. I will do my best to put my worry aside and let Him finish this and bring us home. Three more days - but who's counting!

October 5

Philippians 4:6 - "Do not be anxious about anything, but in everything by prayer and petition, with thanksgiving, present your requests to the Lord."

The verse above is on a ring I bought before coming to Uganda.

Oh, friends, today was a rough day. This is a tough message to write, and my heart is broken. We stopped by the Embassy to pay our visa fees and were told there was some bad news. They are questioning some information regarding the girls' orphan status, which could significantly delay our homecoming.

I am asking for prayer that God will move mountains tomorrow. I know He is in control, and He has a plan. The scary thing is that we don't always see the timing of that plan or how it will all come together. I know for sure that I will bring Fiona home. God has not brought us this far not to. I have said this many times – our battles are best turned over to God. WE NEED HIM TO FIGHT FOR US IN THIS WORLD!

The pastor at church on Sunday talked about the power of God being "supernatural." He is so much bigger than all this. His power and might can change ANY situation. We will give Him all the glory for His work here when this is done. Sending love and gratitude for urgent prayers on our behalf tonight.

The date of this blog post is October 5th. I didn't realize until I was writing this book and got to this spot that this was October 5th, a day so familiar to me. Four years ago, I had my most intimate encounter with God in a hospital room where I called out to Him in all my desperation, and He met me. Four years later to the day, I found myself halfway around the world, again crying out to God in a desperate plea. I wish that on that day in Africa, I would have realized the connection. I wonder if it would have provided me some peace. Unlike the peace that came over me on this day four years ago, this particular October 5th offered none.

Much like my first blog post, there is so much left out of this last post. There was so much I could not share then. So many things about this day and October 5, 2006, were the same. I was in a drastically different world, but the internal war inside me was familiar. The noise was so loud inside of me that I felt there was no escape. My fear of going to the Embassy this day was real. I knew it would not go well, but I tried to pretend otherwise. While putting on a brave front, I think God was preparing me for news I did not want to hear.

I was falling apart, piece by piece, as the day unfolded. I would not be able to share the events of this day without sharing what happened at the Embassy that afternoon. A little behind-the-scenes footage. When the clerk told us there was a problem with the orphan investigation, I proceeded to have a meltdown that exceeded any other meltdown I had ever had. And I had my share over the past few years. I immediately lost it. There was no build-up; it just happened. We were standing in this little room, with enough space for two people to comfortably stand. There is a glass window between the Embassy employee and the person on the other side. Reactions such as this perfectly explain why this partition is there. There is no way to completely describe my response. Picture the actress who has received the worst news in a dramatic scene – they cry, put their back up against the wall and melt to the ground. That is probably the best image I can provide.

I cried; I yelled; I begged; I questioned why. Over and over again. Nothing the clerk said was going to offer me what I needed. Their minds were already made up. I am not sure how much time passed, but the clerk finally said there was nothing else she could do for us that day, and we needed to go. I want to say that I pulled myself together at this point, but I would be lying. On the drive back to the guesthouse, I was inconsolable. Once back, I talked to Dave, standing out on the balcony at the guesthouse, trying to come up with a solution to this mess I was in, but there was nothing. I cried out in total desperation to God that day to rescue me. Unlike that day in 2006, there was silence.

October 6 - We Wait Upon the Lord

These last three days have been tough. I have shed so many tears as I have questioned why we are running into problems at this final stage. I have felt sorry for myself and the decisions that must be made. We were told yesterday that a more extensive orphan investigation was needed; today, we were told it could take up to two weeks to complete. If they are satisfied at the end of that, they will grant the visas. If not, they will send the cases to Nairobi, which could be held up for weeks, at best.

Our flights are scheduled for tomorrow night, and the decision to stay or go has been weighing heavy. Florence, Betty, and Livingstone came to pray with us a while ago. I am always amazed at the faith that these individuals show. When they ask God for something, they ask for it, believing that it has happened.

While I could not understand all the prayers, it did not matter. They were calling on the Lord with no fear - THANKING Him for what he has done repeatedly - and for what He was going to do.

October 7

After a long couple of days of difficult and uncertain news, we decided to extend our stay for one week and see what happens.

Tonight, we hoped we would be on the plane with our girls for our big homecoming tomorrow. I am so frustrated with the process. We have come so far and to be halted at the finish line is heartbreaking. We need to take a step back for a few days, let the process move, and, more importantly, let God work. I need to stand back, get out of the way, and let Him fight this battle for us. He will work all this out in a bigger and better way than we could have imagined, and we will give Him all the glory when that happens.

October 8

It was a long day. Days seem so much longer here. There was no news from the Embassy today. We know some interviews have taken place on the investigation and hope to have some news early in the week.

Rachelle and I have felt at peace today and know God is working. We can feel all the prayers coming on our behalf. I am thankful to talk to family at home and Tyler this morning before school. I am grateful for what God has accomplished here and for what He will do. And I am thankful for my little Fiona sleeping beside me right now. All is good because God is good!

October 9

We came into Kampala today and had lunch with some other moms in-country - we are all in the process of waiting for our visas, so we are not alone here. After that, we took a little break from the guesthouse and checked into a nice hotel in the city for one night. It's got a pool, so the girls really enjoyed that. We had ice cream for dinner and went to the salon to all have pedicures. The girls' expressions were priceless. They looked scared but loved the way they looked afterward. God is in control, and we thank Him for the fun time we've been able to have today.

October 10

We've been here for about a month. Livingstone came over to visit tonight, and we sat for a while and talked about everything that had happened. Some of our paths along this journey have seemed troubled. Yet, as we talked about it, there are so many places where we see God has been orchestrating it all, every meeting, every conversation, He's been in it all.

I have many highlighted verses in my bible that I like to look through when I need some encouraging words. The verse I opened up to tonight is one of my favorites. John 16:33 "I have told you these things, so that in me you may have peace. In this world, you will have trouble. But take heart! I have overcome the world."

God has given us His words so that we may have peace in this world, a world that will sometimes be full of trouble. But have faith, He has overcome the world! I look at this coming week and could worry all day and night about what could happen. What trouble could be around the corner waiting for me? But God has overcome the world, conquered battles, and paved paths that only He could.

October 11

Hebrews 11:1 NIV says, "Now faith is being sure of what we hope for, and certain of what we do not see."

Today was quiet. Lots of time to think, which is sometimes good and sometimes bad. Tonight, Livingstone came over with one of the ministers from church, Jonathan. We went through some scripture together before praying. Like the scripture I quoted last night, he talked about how we will all have trouble in this world but that we should never give up on God's plan. His prayer was perfect as he prayed for everything in my heart.

The waiting is hard, but we are called to wait upon the Lord. One thing I have no doubt in is that Fiona is ours. God will be victorious in this battle. Jonathan said that he believes God is giving us a testimony to share for the rest of our lives. I agree with that. God is giving us a story to tell, and it will be our job to ensure we do just that.

October 12 - Waiting on the Lord

Today was one of the longest days of waiting we have had here. Two and a half weeks ago, when we received our adoption ruling, I thought that was it - the rest would be smooth sailing. Yet, here we are. I could go on all day about my frustrations with this. We are left at a crossroads tonight - one I do not want to be at.

Many of the things pastor Jonathon shared last night have meant a lot to me today. He told us that life is not going to be smooth sailing. Life is going to present us with trouble and problems. He also told us that once God provides a vision, He will see it through to completion, and we are to never give up. There is a victory to come.

We don't know how long it will take to get her visa. Maybe a week, two or three, we don't know. There is literally nothing we can do to make things move faster. We have good friends here who can take care of the girls. They live in a nice, secure home and would be well cared for. I am mentally and emotionally spent. I feel bad saying that when I look at all God has done. This is a challenging process, and when we are here, we live and breathe it every moment of every day.

I ask for prayers tonight for clear direction from God regarding what we need to do. I know God has a plan. That doesn't mean it will be easy, but it does mean that we will finish strong. The pastor last night said we will have a safe landing at the end of this journey. Fiona is ours. God choose her to be with us and us to be with her. God grant me the patience and peace I need right now.

October 13

Sara asked that I provide an update to let everyone know that she and Rachelle are headed home this evening. As you have read from Sara's updates, this was a tough decision to make. She was hopeful that the separation from Fiona would be brief, and she would soon be traveling back to bring Fiona home. As Sara will be en-route for the better part of the next 24+ hours, the next update probably won't be until sometime on Friday. I'm sure Sara will provide details at that time, which I'll leave for her to share.

I will borrow the words of Pastor Jonathan in saying that we eagerly but patiently await a "safe landing" when Fiona is united with her new family. In the meantime, thanks to all for your prayerful dedication throughout this journey.

Love,
Fiona's Aunt Becky

These words were so difficult to write that I had to ask my sister to do it for me. I just could not bear it. I had already come home without Fiona once, and I simply could not believe I was about to do it again.

The morning we left, Rachelle came to my room to talk. She had been praying and felt God telling her all was well. She was reminded of the old hymn, "It Is Well with My Soul." [5] I sang it often as a child growing up in church. She told me she had peace about our decision to go home for now, and she was trying to give me that same reassurance, but I was not feeling it at all. The guilt I had for leaving my daughter a second time was more than I could bear. As I read through the posts from the last few days I was in Uganda during this trip, I try to put myself back in that time. While I knew that God was providing me some peace, I was not in the same place as Rachelle. I clearly remember thinking—this is *not* well with my soul.

---

[5] Horatio Spafford. *It Is Well With My Soul.* Bliss and Sankey, Gospel Hymns No. 2, 1876.

ELEVEN

Letting Go Even More

I lift my eyes to the mountains - Where does my help come from?

My help comes from the Lord, the maker of heaven and earth.

—Psalm 121:1-2

Once I was back home, life was so different than when I had left a few weeks ago. My world had changed once again, and I felt detached from anything normal. Leaving Uganda for the second time without her was more than I could take. I could not put a smile on this time and make it appear that everything was okay. It was not okay. Even though we talked about this hopefully being a short-term wait to go back, I knew that would not be the case deep in my heart. I tried to get back into the groove. I wanted to be there for Tyler to try to make up for lost time with him. I had to throw myself back into work, more out of necessity than a desire to go to work. Since Dave lost his vision, I was the full-time worker in our family, and I needed to work to provide for our family. As much as I tried to make things normal, nothing about it was. I was unsettled in every sense of the word.

In my first blog post below, I talk about how I felt I was in a fog. For the next seven months, I found myself in survival mode, only doing what I absolutely had to do to get through each day. Nothing more. As I reflect on these words, I think it best describes where I was. I will let them tell this part of the story.

October 15

We made it home. I got home about 6:00 last night and was in bed by 8:15. I slept for the next 14 hours and again for most of the day. I feel like I am in a fog here. I did not sleep well the last several days we were in Uganda, and not much on the flights home.

Three weeks ago, we were granted the adoption of Fiona. I never thought I'd sit at home today while she is still there. The decision to come home was difficult, and I did not make it until only hours before leaving for the airport. I kept thinking, how can I come home without her again? While leaving was hard, mentally and emotionally, I am spent. Every day is spent trying to fight something you have little control over. I have to give this to God.

Fiona got settled into their new place. Got to Skype with her today. A few minutes after we talked, Fiona wanted to call back to say goodnight again. I left my laptop there, so we should be able to talk daily.

October 17

I've been home a few days now and am starting to readjust. I watched Tyler play in two of his playoff games this weekend which was great since I missed most of the season. He did an awesome job. They were defeated yesterday in the last minute and a half of the game, so the season is officially over. Glad I made it in time to see him play.

We've been able to Skype with Fiona three out of four days. It is so good to see her, talk to her, and know she is well. It is good to be home, but I wish more than anything she was here.

My heart feels torn between here and there. I am thankful that I am not in control and wish I had some control at the same time. I look at what God has done these past few months in my life, and I am amazed. I spent ten weeks this year in a completely different culture. My eyes have been opened to a whole new world. God has given us new friends and family halfway around the world, teaching us so much about faith. And, God has given us a daughter.

October 19

One year ago tomorrow is the day we first learned about Fiona. The instant we heard about her and looked at her picture, we knew something big was about to happen. Hard to believe in some ways that much time has passed, but in other ways, so much has happened. Although the road has not always been smooth (at least it seems that way to us, to God, it's gone exactly as planned), God has brought us a lot of joy and hope as we have worked towards adopting this little girl. Now a year later, we can say she is ours. God has taken us places we never thought we would go and opened our eyes to a new world. We still have a little way to go to bring her home, but we believe God is fighting on our behalf. When it happens, the timing will be perfect.

October 28

This last week was the roughest of this adoption journey and my life. Last Wednesday, we asked the Embassy for an update. On Thursday morning, we received a message that they sent our case to the USCIS office in Nairobi for further review. This means that a visa will not be issued by them right now. They will review the case and then, once it is approved, send it back to the Embassy to process a visa. This was what we feared the most. Hearing it was being sent to Nairobi was like hearing it was being sent to the Bermuda triangle.

Through a network of adoptive parents, we received information on an attorney who can assist in cases like this. We have now spoken at length. I also talked to a new friend this week who returned to the States a few weeks ago after an extended stay in Uganda and her case being sent to Nairobi. It was so helpful to talk to her and receive encouraging words from someone who has been through the same thing. God has placed some incredible people along the way.

When they review our file, they may decide to approve it right away or ask for additional information, which is the most likely thing to happen. This will take time, as anything with this process has. How long? We really don't know. Several weeks most likely.

My mind has been spinning over the last week, and my emotions have been all over the place. God is good, though, and I have been finding peace and hope again the last couple of days. Last weekend was rough, and Monday, I hit my breaking point. I look at where I am today, three days later, and I can only explain the peace I feel by the grace of God. Your prayers have never been more important to us - we appreciate every one of them.

A verse that has come to my attention several times this week has been 1 Peter 5:7 "Cast all your cares upon the Lord, for He cares for you."

November 19 - One Day at a Time

I am sorry that it has been so long since I have updated everyone. As one can imagine, this has been a difficult time. Most days, I try to figure out how to make it through the day. Dave and I have faced several trials these last few years, all of which were hard to face and get through. This one is different, though. This one is harder. This time it is not about one of us but our daughter.

When I wake up, it is the first thing on my mind; when I go to bed, it is the last thing on my mind. I don't go five minutes throughout the day without it being there. I carry it with me wherever I go, whatever I am doing. I have a heartache that won't go away.

A friend reminded me the other day that nothing happening is a surprise to God. He knows everything that will happen and how this will end. I find comfort in talking to God daily and reading scriptures that give me strength. Somehow, He provides me with what I need to get through each day. He gives me enough light to get through.

2 Corinthians 12:9 says: *"My grace is sufficient for you, for my power is made perfect in weakness."*

Please pray for favor in the eyes of the Nairobi USCIS office handling our case. We pray that God's hand will be most evident. I also ask for prayers for peace. That is something I have struggled with the most. Please pray that we will feel the hand of God and that He will continue to shed his grace and peace on us.

Fiona is doing great. We have video chatted with her several times this week, and she is full of smiles. While it is hard to be away from her, I have been able to be here for Tyler for some memorable moments. *I got to go to open house night at school, where Tyler led me around to each class, and we got to talk to all of his teachers. I am thankful I got to go to Tyler's football banquet the other night and to his team party/dinner on Sunday, where he received a special award. I am also thankful I saw him in his first choir concert at school. All of this does a mom's heart good. He is now a junior higher, growing up so fast in these last three months it blows my mind. He is getting excellent grades, and we are so proud of him.*

December 19 - Hope

I hope this Christmas season finds you well. It has been some time since I have posted an update, mainly because there has not been much to report. The weeks have been long, with little to no news to report. I have shed a lot of tears, and my mind has been so full of worry at times that it's been hard to find a way out. I do see a way out at times. That way out has been through God. I've been learning to depend on God for everything, and I'm finding a dependence on Him that I've not had before. Where I didn't think I could find peace, I have. Days where I could not see hope, He's given it to me. God's been giving me the strength to get through each day. His grace has been abundant.

A verse I have gone to frequently has been Philippians 4:6-7: "Do not be anxious about anything, but in everything, by prayer and petition, with thanksgiving, present your requests to God. And the peace of God which transcends all understanding will guard your hearts and your minds in Christ Jesus."

Tonight, I actually have some news to share. Finally, we are hearing from Nairobi, and they are hoping to be able to update us on our case early this week. Since this week is the week of Christmas, we are hoping and praying for good news. It would be an unforgettable Christmas gift to learn we can finally bring Fiona home. Please pray that whatever we learn this week, our hearts will be protected, and we will continue to be filled with peace. We look forward to the day when God's glory will be revealed to all in this situation.

January 14 - No Cure for a Mother's Love

A few weeks after I got home, I was at the doctor's office for a checkup. He asked me to fill him in on things. As I told him about our struggles, I got a little teary - no surprise for those who know me well. He looked and me and said, "There is no cure for a mother's love." And, there isn't. As we've gone through the past twelve weeks since I have been home, it's been a journey of its own. At first, it was an emotional roller coaster. Then I was in fighting mode - gathering everything we could that would help in case we needed it. Now, it's quiet. All of our busy work is done, and we are waiting.

God has given me strength and peace to get through some really tough times, and the neat thing is, the more time passes, the more peace I have that she will soon be home with us. The longer she is away, though, the more and more I miss her. She is such a beautiful little soul, and I cannot wait to share her. My heart hurts. What my doctor said is so true - there is no cure for a mother's love. This heartache I have will not go away until she is here. So, I am trying to live with it knowing it is only temporary. I don't know why we have to wait; maybe we will never know. What I know is that the joy that will come when we bring her home will be bigger and better than we can imagine.

January 14 was the last blog post I wrote while we were waiting. It would be another four months before we would receive the news we had waited for. It's tough to fully describe where I was during that time. Reading back over my posts, I see times when I was able to find hope. I remember those times, and while I believed it, each day was still a challenge. Trying to make it one day at a time turned into trying to make it one minute at a time. Some days I was able to handle my life, go to work, take care of things at home, and be there for Tyler. Other days, I could not do it. A few days I showed up for work, and within a short time, I realized I wasn't going to be able to function, and I'd leave. Every time I opened my email, my anxiety would spike as I waited to see if there was any word. If there was an email from our attorney, I would immediately panic, wondering what it said and if it would be good or bad news. I was never, ever relaxed.

As the end of each day approached, I would find myself restless, my anxiety building. Every evening, there would come the point where I would look at Dave and Tyler and tell them I was going upstairs to have my time with God. For the next couple of hours, I would talk to God. Day by day, I learned to tear down my walls and share every last doubt, fear, or worry on my mind with Him. Somehow as I gave my burdens over to Him, peace would slowly come over me, and my prayers would turn to praises.

During this time, God was my only source of peace. There was nothing else, no one else, that could provide me any source of peace. It was only Him. Everyone around me was trying to help. They all gave their love, support, and prayers. They were doing all they could. But I had reached a point that what I needed could only come from Him. Each day, I found myself depending on God for every single thing I needed. I was entirely dependent on God. He was my source of everything. He is the reason I survived.

I learned there is a hole inside each of us that can only be filled with God. We try to fill that hole with other things. Our family and friends try to put us back together and make us whole. At times, we even expect them to somehow make that happen. We look at things from this world to fill it, to make us feel good for a time. It became clear to me during this season that God is the only one who can fill that emptiness. We are created that way. During these four months, I kept to myself much of the time. It was hard for me to explain to others what I was feeling. I know I was not easy to be around either, as people would tell me it was hard to see me that way.

Dave has always wanted to fix things for me. I tell him something is upsetting me, and he immediately goes into action, trying to think of a possible solution. For Dave, he believed the entire time we would bring Fiona home. I did too, but he and I handled it so differently. I found myself frustrated at the fact that he could compartmentalize it so well. He could still function and go on, being at peace that the answer would come. And I know I sometimes frustrated him because he could not understand why I could not rest and know it would all work out. He gladly gave me the time I needed to be with God at the end of each day. He learned that was the answer for me.

During my time with God, I kept a personal journal. Every day I wrote down my prayers to God. Sometimes I could not keep up trying to write down everything racing around in my mind. I humbled myself before Him each time. I poured everything out. Every thought, every worry, every question. Every feeling of failure or guilt I was holding onto. Most of those journal entries I leave between God and me. I do want to share a few things that I wrote. I mentioned that many times my prayers would turn to praises. I had never really experienced prayer in that way before. I don't know if I had ever praised him to this degree either. At the end of my list of prayer requests, I would start writing down my praises. Below are some of the words I wrote. I read them now and am in awe that these words came from a place of deep pain. That while I was in the darkest place I could imagine, God was able to lift me to a place of praise. Daily restoring my hope.

Jesus is my one true source of peace, comfort, and rest.
When confusion, doubt, anger, and sadness enter,
you call out to me through the storm, telling me you still love me.
When I lack faith, you remind me you are in control.
When I search for answers, you tell me you already know my needs.
When my heart is breaking, you come to my rescue.
When the enemy is attacking, you are my defender and helper.
When I try to find peace here on earth, you remind me
you are my only true source of this.
I tell myself you are in control.

After so much time hurting, I find rest in you.
You are my peace, my light in the darkness, my shelter in the storm,
my refuge in trouble, my protector when I
fear, my defender when attacked.
I hold fast to your promise Lord.
I look for the joy that is coming and dream
of the celebration that is near.
I look to the victory that will be yours,
your glory that will be revealed.
The joy that comes from your victories outweighs the pain;
It makes the journey worth taking.
When I follow your path, I am walking towards you.
You are good, Lord.
I am your child.
You never said the road would be easy, but
you promised to stay with me.
You used this time to show me I still have things to learn.
You showed me the dependence I can have in you alone.
I won't be able to tell my story without you, Lord.
You have given me a story to share.

I can't read those words without a wave of emotions coming over me. Those words did not come to me overnight. My daily prayers lifted to Him over several months brought me to these conclusions. I was learning to praise in the storm. These promises are now tucked away safely in my heart. They are part of me.

Psalm 46:11 NIV: He says, "Be still, and know that I am God; I will be exalted among the nations, I will be exalted in the earth."

In my waiting, this was the lesson to be learned, the truth to fully embrace. He is God; He is all I need. He will take the lead and fight the fight; He will provide. All I need is to be still. In those final months of waiting, I learned to be still. I had to kneel at the cross and surrender. I had to rest in knowing God was fighting the battle. Believing He would be victorious.

TWELVE

It's Over

And the God of all grace, who called you to his eternal glory in Christ, after you have suffered a little while, will himself restore you and make you strong, firm and steadfast.

—1 Peter 5:10

On May 6, 2011, the wait was over. The attorney that we had been working with called my phone. I was at work and heard my cell phone ring. I swung around in my chair to see the phone and her number on the screen. We had been in an endless waiting mode for news from Nairobi that our visa was approved. I anxiously picked up the phone to hear her voice. After saying hello, the first words she said were, "It's over." I will never forget the way those words felt. Very soon, I would be able to travel to Uganda to bring Fiona home.

May 16

When I titled our blog Bringing Fiona Home, I could have never realized the full meaning that phrase would come to mean to us. What a journey this has been. Times of sadness beyond what I thought I could endure and moments of joy I will forever hold in my heart. Those times of joy have gotten me through this last year - promises from God telling me He would see this through. And, He is. In a few days, I will again find myself in Africa. This time - to finally Bring Fiona Home.

May 20

Just finishing day one in Africa, and all is well. Arrived very late last night - close to 1:00 a.m. Our flight was rerouted to Rwanda before coming to Entebbe, adding about three hours to an already long leg of the trip. Staying at a great place - the best so far - with a fellow adoptive mom friend. Got to see Fiona this morning, and she ran into my arms with a big smile. The last seven months of our lives have been full of heartache, waiting and praying for this to come. I can't believe it, but that heartache is somehow already fading. God is good! Went to finish her medical report this morning, and all was good. Then we all went to lunch, and since it is Friday, we made the trip to the market. Love to you all, and can't wait to see everyone back home next week. Until then, I am going to soak in the goodness here.

May 22

We started off this Sunday with a trip to church. Worship was fabulous as always. Then we visited Mama Scovia's house, where we saw many of our favorite kids we had not seen in a long time. They are all so sweet and greeted us with hugs and smiles. It feels so good to be back here with Fiona knowing I will soon be bringing her home. Tomorrow night we are having a big dinner party with all the special people who have become family through this process. Looking forward to celebrating with our dear friends.

Tomorrow is the day we have been waiting for - our trip to the Embassy. It is hard not to feel a little anxious about going there. As I have told many people, the last time I was there, I probably had the biggest meltdown of my life, so it does not hold the fondest memories for me. God has brought us on this journey and had a plan. Each trial has brought us closer to Him, and he continues to reveal His goodness. This time, He has given us our daughter.

May 23

Today was another eventful day. We hoped to have our visa in hand. However, since a new medical was required (done and in their hands) since the old one had expired, we were told they needed a little extra processing time. We were told we could come back on Wednesday to pick it up, but as you all know, we fly home tomorrow night. In the end, and to keep a long story short and simple for now, they told us to come back tomorrow to pick it up. This will mean that we will most likely go to the airport right from the Embassy.

Tonight, we had dear friends over for a big dinner party. The house was packed. Everyone enjoyed a traditional Ugandan meal, talked, sang, and prayed together. What an amazing group of people who we now call family. Goodbyes are not easy, though, and I admit I had to fight back the tears more than once, not knowing when we will see them again. Uganda and these individuals have changed who I am and how I look at the world. What a gift.

Tomorrow we will pack up, head back to the Embassy, and then the airport. I hope I do not feel like I am on an Amazing Race episode, but that may happen. Your continued prayers over these next 24 hours are greatly appreciated.

We look forward to seeing everyone soon and introducing you to the newest Brodzinski. Look out, world!

May 30

Finally, Home! It's been a long wait, but more than worth it to finally have our girl home with us. We got home Wednesday night and were greeted at the airport in Chicago by our family. It was so great for Fiona and Tyler to finally meet in person. Fiona is quite fond of her big brother, and Tyler is quite fond of her. He has been very attentive to her - so sweet.

On Thursday, we made a quick visit to the school and were able to pick up her registration forms for next year. Every morning since then, she wakes up and tells me, "I am going to my school today!"

On Saturday, we headed to Indianapolis for a family reunion, in time to welcome the newest Brodzinski. It had been a long time since we had so much of the family together; it was a lot of fun. On Sunday, we got to go to church - our church has been praying for this day to come for a long time now - so it was so great to finally be there! Last night we went to a party with some of Dave's family. It was cold and rainy, but that didn't stop Fiona from wanting to play in the little kiddie pool and splash around. Today we are headed to the local Memorial Day parade and then to my parents for a cookout. It should be a fun day.

It is incredible to finally have our girl home. She is taking everything in and seems comfortable in her new home. She loves her pink room and sleeps there all night by herself (she has never had her own room or slept alone, but she seems okay with it). On her second night home, she woke up at 3:30 a.m. calling for me. I went there, and she informed me, "I am done sleeping." I told her she still had a couple of hours to go. I think there is too much to explore here, and sleep is a waste of time. On her first night home, when we were putting her to bed, she looked at Dave and asked, "Daddy, is there a swimming pool here?" She is all girl. She is sweet, full of smiles, and so funny. Our house is much busier with a lively six-year-old running around - she seems to have boundless energy. She has her whole family wrapped around her finger, and seeing the world through her eyes is fun!

We praise God for Bringing Fiona Home!

Bringing Fiona Home was a life-changing experience in every way possible. From the moment we saw her face on our computer screen to the airplane wheels lifting off the ground, every single experience shaped our lives. It's completely changed how we want to live the rest of our lives. I clearly remember feeling God was preparing me for something big when I was sick. When I think of our time in Uganda and everything we went through, I also had the clear sense that something bigger would come from this. And it did.

THIRTEEN

Do Not Be Afraid

Have I not commanded you, be strong and courageous? Do not be afraid, do not be discouraged, for the Lord your God will be with you wherever you go.

—Joshua 1:9

I met Dave on my 19th birthday. I was a cashier at the local grocery store, the same store where I buy my weekly groceries today. He was a bagger. It was a grocery store romance like none other. From the second we met, I liked him and soon learned he liked me too as he found his way over to my lane to bag groceries as often as he could. Within a couple of weeks, he got the nerve up to ask me, and I said yes. The rest is history. In a short time, I could see this was the man I would marry. Anyone who knew us back then would say we were meant for each other. And they would be right. On August 6, three years later, we were married. My grandfather was a minister, and many moons before this day, he baptized my twin sister and me at his small country church, Bethel. On this day, he married us. I feel blessed that my grandpa played a significant role in both events.

There are certain memories in life that stay alive like they just happened. The day he married us contained one of those, many in fact, but one in particular that came from him. After we were pronounced husband and wife, he was about to introduce us as Mr. and Mrs. to the audience. He paused and, in his sweet grandpa voice, said, "Today, I am the happiest grandpa on God's green earth." His voice held such emotion that it had to capture every heart there. As a granddaughter who knew how special that was, it forever captured mine.

Young and in love, we had no idea what our lives would hold. We started out in a little apartment with only the things we needed. It seems like a lifetime ago. Since then, our lives have taken so many unexpected turns that Dave chose to look at our life as an adventure early on. He tries not to focus on the challenges but on how we have overcome those challenges with God. Dave did not grow up attending church but came with me when we started dating. As the years passed, he began to feel very much at home with God. Several years into our marriage, he officially gave his life to Jesus. He was baptized at the same church where we'd been married. Over time, I guess one could say God made himself comfortable there in Dave's heart, and He began to grow in his life until He was part of his being. Dave undeniably loves Jesus. He will tell any person, at any time, without hesitation that he loves Jesus. And, he will gladly share why he loves Jesus with the other person because he wants the same for them. This ability to share God with others did not come overnight. It came from years of God molding and shaping his heart, using every experience he went through to build that courage that now lives in him. And it keeps growing.

Many of us spend a great deal of time building up and tearing down the walls around us. Sometimes, we let Jesus in. Other times, we keep ourselves busy laying bricks. Dave did this, too, for many years. For the past few years, however, his walls came down brick by brick, and he's managed to let God in daily. That's not to say an occasional brick or two isn't laid once again, but allowing the walls to crumble has changed his life in many ways. Above all, I see an acceptance of his blindness that I didn't think I would ever see. The man I was married to a few years ago, with walls built high around him, is strikingly different than the man I am married to today.

We have been married for close to three decades. During the first half of our life together, I was married to a man who could see. In the second half, I was married to a man who fought blindness until he lost all of his vision.

Our life together has not been easy. I wish some things were different, that certain things could have just been easier. I am reminded, however, that we are who we are because of the journey. And where we are today would not look at all like today had we not taken the twists and turns we did. Dave loves to look back at what we've been through and dreams about where we will go. To him, it's all a compilation of adventures God has laid out for us. Even though our life together has been challenging, here is one thing I know—when God chose Dave for me, he gave me a man who will eternally love me. Even when I am hard to love. At the end of the day, I never doubt his love and never will. I call that blessed.

Joshua 1:9 says, "Have I not commanded you, be strong and courageous. Do not be afraid, do not be discouraged, for the Lord your God will be with you wherever you go."

This is a verse that Dave keeps close to his heart. It came into his life at an uncertain time. He grabbed hold of it and found hope in its message.

Since his surgery in 2009, the next several years yielded several more. All attempts to slow down the loss of his vision. Each one, however, did not hold the outcome we were looking for. His eye refused to cooperate the way the doctors wanted it to. Each surgery, which we hoped would bring improvement or even stabilize his vision, brought disappointment. His loss of vision came in waves. Things would be going along perfectly fine, and then suddenly, his vision would change, and we knew something was up. Like the ocean's waves, the aftermath would crash around us without warning. Each time, his vision decreased enough that he had to readjust to a new reality. It felt like a never-ending cycle.

Remember how I said that some people shared that it was hard for them to watch me going through the waiting to bring Fiona home? I now understood what they meant. When we got married all those years ago, we knew there was a chance he could lose his sight. I thought it would be much later in life if it were to happen. I recall a time when I didn't worry about it happening. I thought we had so much time before we'd have to face it or if we would ever have to. And, if it happened someday, it would be okay. We would figure it out.

Like most things, it's impossible to see the gravity of a situation until it is happening. While I have stood by Dave and will continue to all my days, I would be lying if I said this was not the most difficult of things to watch and experience. I have seen his fear, watched his frustration, experienced his sadness for losing what he once had, and the anger he has had to battle. I've seen depression engulf him. There were days that he was better able to accept what was happening. And there were days when it tore him apart. He spent years fighting becoming blind; it was all-consuming. He lived and breathed it every second of every day. Trying to understand and accept what was happening, knowing it was entirely out of his control.

While we were fighting his blindness, life was constantly changing. Changing for him. Changing for me. For a long time, I was not able to admit that. I could readily concede it to myself. My life was changing in ways I had never imagined. The problem with admitting it to others was the guilt I felt. I couldn't make this about me. I was not the one going blind; it was my job to help and support him through this loss. The reality was, though, it was happening to me. The day came when I had to start admitting that. I fought it for many reasons, but under all the layers, I didn't want to admit or accept it because once I did, I would have to accept that our lives were forever changed. There would be no going back to the way things were. This was our new reality. Dave was losing his vision, and I was losing it too.

I am grateful to say that we have come a long, long way. I can also admit that it's not over. While most days we have learned to live in our new world, there are times and days when frustration or sadness sneaks back in and brings us down. Writing about Dave's blindness has been by far the most challenging part of my story to tell. I think that is because we are still living it. It's a part of our daily existence that will not go away. Even though we are years into this, we are each still learning how to navigate our lives with it.

We all face trials that we don't want to confront. We fight in different ways. Dave and I fought his blindness in different ways.

We each sought to control a situation we had no control over. This eventually led us to a point where we had to decide between control and surrender.

The definition of surrender is to yield to the power of another. As a Christian, it is about relinquishing control. Taking it out of our hands and putting it in His hands. It's something I've hung onto so tight at times that it doesn't make sense. I know, and I've experienced surrendering to God, putting my problems into his most capable and powerful hands. I've seen the goodness and freedom that come from surrender. I know, yet I forget, how powerful God is. God has helped me, and yet I refuse to hand certain things over to Him when that is what I am being called to do.

I want to share some things I have had to accept and surrender. One of those is the feeling that I am alone. I didn't want to let anyone into my life deep enough to see what was happening behind the scenes for a long time. I have felt alone because I am the only person I know married to someone who is blind. How could anyone possibly relate to this? I felt unseen. People would ask Dave how he was doing. They would tell Dave how brave or optimistic he remained with losing sight. Dave was and is brave and, as I have shared, remarkably optimistic. I saw a Dave that no one else did, however. I saw him in constant states of frustration as he relearned his world. I witnessed the anger over what was happening to him. I saw the fear that made him want to say no to the next step or say he couldn't when it was something he needed to do. I experienced the pain and the sadness that lived in his heart more often than I could take. I saw him desperately trying to find a way out of his circumstances. I wanted to take those things from him. I tried to ease the burden. I have spent much of my life wanting to spare others from their feelings. I want to take it from them so they won't have to hurt. I would never claim to understand what it's like to be him, but I can say that I have carried some of his fear, sadness, anxiety, and even anger with me.

It was hard to share how I felt about it because no one could truly relate. So, I thought. I have learned people understand more than I gave them credit for by sharing what is in my heart. The more I opened up to my friends and family, the more they saw my heart and understood. The more we let people in, the more we learned they wanted to help somehow. They also, because they cared for us, wanted to carry some of the burden so we would not have to. I realized that I didn't need someone to fully understand it. People are going through all sorts of things that I will never understand. We can be there for one another, share the love and hope of Jesus, give them an ear to listen, and share unconditional love as they share their story. Regardless of what we understand about another person's reality, we have so much to offer.

Dave and I have fought the feeling of not wanting to be different. This was a tough one for Dave. He did everything he could to hide his blindness. When he was working at our church, people would learn he was blind and be shocked. They had no idea, and that is how he wanted it. He went to great lengths to hide it. He would promise to coordinate activities, gather supplies, go shopping, set up events; the list went on and on. People did not know we would go into the church on Saturdays to walk the paths he would take on Sunday mornings. If he was going to make announcements on the church stage, we would practice going up the steps and standing where he would stand so that his blindness would go unnoticed.

As time passed, it became harder and harder to mask. We were both becoming buried, taking on endless tasks to cover up what was happening in our lives. The more challenging things got with his vision, the harder he worked to cover it up. When we look back at that time, we relate him to being a bull in a China shop. He was going to do whatever it took, full speed ahead, without regard to the collateral damage, which was usually me.

The weight on my shoulders of being responsible for each step he took outside of our home was tremendous. Every step, every curb, every doorway, obstacle, or turn. I was in charge of every step. He would be frustrated and embarrassed when we accidentally missed a curb or ran into something not gauging the situation correctly. I would find myself wanting to shrink as people watched us. There was no place we went where eyes were not on us. It felt like so much pressure at the time. It was overwhelming. Dave fought the idea of using a white cane because that would finally be the point where he could no longer hide his vision loss. Reaching a breaking point, while sitting at lunch one day, I told him I had ordered him a white cane and that he would start using it. Even though I was his favorite crutch, the time came to research better long-term solutions so he could live life more independently.

We started thinking about applying for a Leader Dog for the blind. Early in that process, the Leader Dog organization told him that he would first need to come to their orientation and mobility training. This required him to go to their facility for a week by himself to work with trainers. It was an enormous step for him, knowing he would be pushed far outside his comfort zone. Going to the training was a huge turning point, leading to many other good things. After he was home from training, we started the official application for a leader dog.

Within a few months of applying, a seventy-five-pound black lab named Flynn walked into our lives. He soon found himself back at the leader dog facility, this time for close to a month, where he and Flynn trained side by side. Today, there is not a place we go where we don't make friends. A trip to the grocery, the hardware store, the bank, or out to eat always has us meeting people eager to talk and ask questions. Do we sometimes feel on display? Absolutely! I'd be lying if I said otherwise. But our lives become richer as we talk with people. We are sharing our story, and before we know it, they are sharing their story, something they have been through that makes them different from everyone else. That is something we would not want to change for anything.

With Flynn, Dave can no longer hide his blindness. Instead, it puts it front and center. This dog is special. That is what I tell everyone. Of course, I am biased, but he really, really is. His seventy-five pounds of pure goodness and love have made grown men cry in public. God created Flynn to be Dave's partner because he knew that Dave would witness to people and share his testimony. I swear this dog also knows he is working for the Lord. One of Dave's worries about being blind was how he would start conversations with people, and Flynn is the open door that allows all of that to happen and more.

We've learned that being different, while challenging, can also bring opportunities. A wise pastor explained to Dave one day that he could look at his blindness as a loss or use it as a testimony. Once he realized that he could turn this loss into a way of reaching people, his mindset began to change.

As I have shared, I do believe God joined us. He intended for us to spend our lives together. Admittedly, life, and in this case married life, has not been easy. Why didn't someone warn us that marriage would be hard and require a lot of work? Maybe a few did. At the time, though, we couldn't see that far ahead. The truth is I have been married to a man who could see, and I've been married to a man who can't see. He knows what he had and what he doesn't have now. And, I know what I had then and what I have now. A new reality has replaced an old reality. That is not all bad. In fact, it truly is good; I can say that with a sincere heart. We've grown beyond what we could have envisioned and seen beauty in the midst of pain. That did not happen quickly, though.

We have not always given each other the best version of ourselves. When life was crashing around us, we tended to give each other the broken pieces that remained. Blindness has changed every aspect of our lives, meaning that every part of our lives felt broken at one point or another. We wondered if life would ever feel normal again. I would see normal people doing everyday things and feel like I had been cheated out of a normal life. I realize there is no such thing as normal, and everyone has a story that others can't see. But—when you are in the mud, you are in the mud.

To be completely real, I was jealous of the normalness I

thought others had. I can still find myself in that mindset. There are things I simply miss about my husband who could see. There are things I long to have back that I will never get back. And learning to accept some of those things has made my heart ache. It still aches. The thing that I miss more than anything is looking in his eyes and having him see me back. Out of all the things I miss, this is a tough one for me to surrender. The ability to communicate without words has been taken from us.

I never realized all the things we said to each other with just a look. I never fully realized until it was gone the comfort that it brought me to look in his eyes and have him understand me. I miss seeing the way he would look at me that would undoubtedly tell me he loved me at a glance. To have to put into words the things that I used to be able to communicate with a look is something challenging for me. I shared earlier how he loved to watch Tyler. He would take in everything about him. Dave did the same with me. So often, I would feel I was being watched and glance over to find him happily looking at me. I'd ask what he was doing and say something like he was taking it all in or tell me that I was beautiful. He loved to comment about the spark I would get in my eyes when talking about something I loved. He still tells me I am beautiful and reminds me that he will always remember me without wrinkles or gray hair. I know he still believes I am beautiful, but oh, how I wish he could see me when he is saying it. And perhaps strangely, I am sad that he won't see me grow old.

While my life was changing with Dave losing his sight, our kids' lives were changing too. For Fiona, she never had a fully sighted dad, but she witnessed the decline. Tyler can remember a dad who could run and play with him, drive a car, and go on outings with just the two of them. He remembers a dad who could watch him play baseball. Tyler's favorite thing to do when he was young was to have Dave throw the baseball to him so he could practice his batting. If it wasn't a baseball, they would be throwing the football back and forth for as long as Dave's arm could keep throwing. They would go until it was dark outside, and I loved watching them spend this time together as I could see how much it meant to our boy.

As time went on, throwing the baseball became a real challenge. Dave could fake it if he knew exactly where Tyler was standing. There came a time, though, when it was no longer possible. I remember one evening so vividly. All four of us were out back. Fiona and I sat on the patio while Dave and Tyler tried to throw the ball and practice hitting. Dave's accuracy was declining, and while Tyler had shown patience up to this point, he also reached his breaking point. His frustration was building as he kept asking Dave to try one more time. Tyler eventually broke down. He was so angry at the situation and so sad.

Everything he'd been packing away inside of him came bursting out all at once. While I could see what was happening, Dave did not. Before I knew it, things were just out of control in all directions. Real life blew up without warning that night. Tyler cried for hours. Fiona quietly observed all of it. Dave was worked up over the blow-up, not understanding it and thinking Tyler was just throwing a fit. As for me, my heart was aching for my boy, who had just realized what he was losing. With that, I was left to be there for each of them because that's what wives and moms do.

I wish I could say that was the only emotional outburst in our family while Dave was losing his vision. However, it certainly was not. We each took our turns becoming emotional, experiencing the fear, the frustration, the hurt, the anger, and the sadness of what was happening to our world. Just as husbands and wives don't always get the best version of themselves to each other, moms and dads don't always give their kids the best versions of themselves either.

Why do I share this? Because life is not pretty. This is real life regardless of what others would like to tell you or what social media would like to portray. Again, I tell you—you are not alone. There was a lot of healing to be done in our family. Some of that healing is still taking place. Ultimately, we all love each other and are a real, true family in every sense. We stick with each other, have the hard conversations, and unconditionally love one another even when that is not the easiest thing to do.

Surrender. That is where we started in this chapter. Many people will say that time heals. I believe that it is God who heals. Surrendering to Him allows Him time and space to work in our lives. Surrender allows us to listen with a new ear. Surrender will allow Him to give us a new perspective on life, letting us see things in a brand-new light. Dave spent so much time worrying that he was losing his credibility by losing sight. He felt that his thoughts or ideas were losing value. God has shown him that he is credible. God has given him a unique testimony to share that speaks to people in a new way. Surrender has allowed this to happen.

We spent so much time for so many years praying for the

vision itself that we missed praying for God to help us regardless of the outcome. Our small group family who walked with us pointed this out one night. It became a turning point in how we prayed about things. His blindness does not have control over him like it once did. He found peace with God and something more significant to fight for in this world.

I hope you are starting to grasp this truth; you are not alone. We are human, and we feel things, good or bad. God created us and our emotions that go along with living in this world. He did not create emotions and expect us to not feel them. However, He wants us to seek Him by letting our emotions guide us to Him for the help we need.

Dave's ambitions rarely took a break regardless of what life was throwing at us. In 2014, Dave started his Master's degree. He crossed the finish line five years later with a Master's in Christian Ministry. So many roadblocks were put in his way. In the midst of it, there were times I wanted him to take a break from it for both of our sakes. Working on his Master's while trying to learn how to do that without sight meant that I followed him throughout that entire process. Surgeries caused him to momentarily stop and rest. His loss of vision made him pause so that he could learn new computer software that would allow him to continue. We continually sought God to fill us with the strength we needed to take the next step. During the last couple of classes for his ministry degree, Dave was tasked with writing his testimony. I believe the assignment came at precisely the right time. In his testimony, he shared that even with the loss of his physical sight, God gave him a new vision he never had. One that allows him to see the world differently and causes him to take action. As his wife, I can confirm he truly believes that. For so long, I didn't think that would ever be possible. The fact that he can say that now and genuinely means it is a victory for Jesus.

We have come a long way. The race is not over though. We will continue to live with his blindness for the rest of our days. Let me leave this thought that has carried me through. While Dave's sight may be lost in the earthly world, he will gain new sight in eternity. His sight may fail him in the flesh, but God will restore his sight one day. There will be a day where everything will be seen, and God's glory will be unveiled. Dave will enjoy the depth and the beauty of God's creation. We are here for a breath; we will be with Him for eternity.

Isaiah 35:5 says,
"Then will the eyes of the blind be opened
and the ears of the deaf unstopped."

FOURTEEN

The Good News

And He said to them go into all the world and proclaim the gospel to the whole creation.

—Mark 16:15

The challenge in this world of chaos and distraction is to keep our eyes focused on Him. To keep our eyes on the cross. To keep our ears listening to Him. Keep our hearts open and available to the call He has placed on our hearts.

For a long time, I have procrastinated and postponed accomplishing the call he put on my heart to share my story. I return to that fear and see the control it still has on me. I am trying to break free. I'm trying to break the chains that keep me from leaping into this next chapter of life. Fear and doubt of my own capabilities encourage me to hit the pause button all too often. It's not that I don't believe in what I am writing. It's that I will have to allow myself to be vulnerable enough to share it with anyone who wants to pick it up and read it. So often, too often, I bank on my own abilities to make things happen. I do this fully aware that there is One who will provide everything I may lack. One who wants to freely give me all I need to succeed and accomplish His work for me. He is saying, come, let me lead; show you the way to a life that is so big and so full; a life where you will feel more alive than ever. Where your heart is on fire for Me. I want to continue to open your eyes to the world. Open your heart to the people that need the hope only I can bring. I want you to share that. Fully give yourself to me, and you will find abundant life. The meaningful life you long for. Cast your fears on me, and I will cast them aside.

I listen to a lot of Christian music. I have found that I have to. It helps to keep my thoughts focused on Him. Many songs talk about how God does not need us but wants us. God does not need us; He is the Almighty! But still, He wants us. Like lost sheep, the shepherd looks for each last one to bring home. Knowing He wants us and will use us for His purpose, with our flaws and scars and doubts and fears, is evidence of His love.

I go back to God's call—share your story. So, I will allow my confidence, which comes solely from Him, to overcome the fear that holds me back from sharing the good news of Jesus.

The more God works on my heart, the more I want others to experience the same. The more He opens the world to me, the more I desire to see. I think about the mark I want to leave on this world. What I want to be remembered for. What will people say when they are called to speak about my life. I want them to quickly be able to say, she lived for God. I don't want it to be for what I have accomplished on my own; I want it to be about what I did through and for God. Of course, I want to be remembered for my love of family and friends. But I also want to be remembered as someone who deeply cared for other people and shared the good news of Jesus. Who boldly lived for God and accepted His mission to be a disciple in this world of lost and broken people. I want to be seen as someone who took action and allowed God to guide my steps. I pray that the things of this world that hold me down will be lifted from me.

I talked about my grandfather earlier. His name was Gerald. He was a one-of-a-kind guy. He loved Jesus and lived his life for Him. For my grandpa, it was a simple and clear calling in his life. For the 27 years, I was graced with his presence on this earth, I never heard him say a bad word about anyone. Ever. It wasn't who he was. He loved Jesus, and he loved people. And he gave his life to others. At his funeral, I was pregnant with Tyler, so pregnant and uncomfortable and unaware that he would enter this world in a couple of days. My grandfather left this world on a Sunday, and on the following Sunday, Tyler entered this world. I like to think that their souls crossed paths. Sitting at his funeral, I listened to people speak of his life dedicated to God. They played one of my favorite songs, "Thank You." Some of the words to that song are, "Thank you for giving to the Lord, I am a life that was changed. Thank you for giving to the Lord, I am so glad you gave."[6] The perfect song for a life so well lived. He is an inspiration to me, as he was to so many.

All of my grandparents have been a blessing to me. Each one brought something special to my life. They have all now gone on to be with the Lord. Every once in a while, one of them will appear in my dreams. Each one makes their own special appearance for me. They always come at the right time. When my grandma Juanita is in my dreams, she is always laughing. That woman loved to talk, and she loved to laugh. I know she continues to this day. So, on special occasions, I will find her in my dreams, and we share a laugh. She was married to my grandpa Gerald.

---

[6] Raymond H. Boltz. *Thank You*. Track 2 on Thank You. Steve Millikan, Word Distribution, 1994.

She was the loyal minister's wife who sacrificed and supported him throughout his calling on earth. She was full of joy and loved living life. Time spent with her was a gift. She loved her family to the fullest, and we never left her wondering what we meant to her. She gave the best hugs. She would wrap us up in her arms. She was always breaking out in a sweat, so this cool dampness always came with her hugs. When she passed, one of the things I missed the most were those hugs. What I wouldn't give for one more of her cool, damp hugs.

My grandpa Gerald has also shown up in my dreams. One night when we were waiting for things to work out in Uganda, I was having a particularly tough day. That night, my grandpa showed up. He was standing at the end of a long, dark hallway, with a light coming from behind him. He stood there so quietly, which was exactly like him. He didn't say anything, but as I got closer to him, his arms were open for me. He wrapped his arms around me, and I woke up. As I woke up, I could feel his arms wrapped around me. I believe God sent him to me in that way to let me know everything was going to be ok.

The day my grandpa Houston was called home, I sat with him most of the day. As time passed, he started asking for his sunglasses. It seemed so strange at the time. The blinds were drawn in the little pink bedroom where his hospital bed sat in his last days. He lay wearing his dark sunglasses, complaining it was still so bright. I don't know how I didn't see it at the time. He was on his way home. As he was called in those final hours, the light was so bright that even on this side of heaven, he needed his sunglasses. I treasure these little glimpses of the home that awaits us.

Recently, I lost my grandma Helen. Having had her in my life for 49 years, we lived a lot of life together. At 95, she was always there, and it's hard to imagine it any other way. In her final two weeks, we knew God was about to call her home. I feel blessed that I was able to spend so much time with her in her final days and for the talks we had about how she was going to meet Jesus and be reunited with loved ones. We imagined what that would be like and what grandpa Houston would say when he welcomed her home. She was ready to go; her life was lived until it was complete. I have thought about this since her passing; how many people live their lives and are ready when the time comes to go home? She pulled out so many old memories in her last days, some of which we could recall and others brand new. She kept remembering when she was in a class, and when the teacher did roll call for the first time, each student had to stand and share a favorite verse. She recalled how she was nervous when her time came, but then a scripture came to her, and she recited it word for word. It was Psalm 19:14, which says, "May the words of my mouth and the meditation of my heart be pleasing to you O Lord, my rock and my redeemer." She vividly remembered how God provided those words for her. She shared this particular memory several times in her final days, and I have continued to wonder what it was about that memory that kept coming to her mind. Whenever something like this is repeated several times, I feel God is trying to get my attention. He wants me to take hold of what is being said.

We live in a world of what seems to be endless darkness. With that, I see a world desperately in need of Jesus. Behind the noise that fills our minds, the conflict, harsh words, and criticism is a need for Jesus, who makes all of these unnecessary. We have a choice to make every day about how we are going to receive this world. All more critical that we focus our minds and meditations on God so that when the world tries to pull us away, we will be reminded of where our thoughts should remain.

Will we fight darkness with darkness? Or will we fight darkness with the light? I know what will happen in the end because God has already promised us that the darkness will eventually be overcome by the light. But in the meantime, in a world where it sometimes seems everyone is looking for something to be against, negativity leads us to be disillusioned that there is no good. I want to be someone who is looking for something to be for. Someone to be for. The power of His light is much greater than anything in this world. My simple and pure plea is that each person finds something to be for. Someone to share the good news with. Ways to share the light and God's love.

I pray we can all put our fears aside and receive God's call on our lives. To recognize and accept that we don't have to have the answers or be qualified. He will provide all that is needed and more. A life lived with a dependence on Him is the way God always intended it to be.

"Be a light for all to see."
Matthew 5:16

FIFTEEN

Our Mission Is On

Then I heard the voice of the Lord saying, "Whom
shall I send? And who will go for us?"
And I said, "Here am I. Send me!"

—Isaiah 6:8

After learning about Fiona and knowing our lives were about to change unexpectedly, our friends gave us a book to read called, The Hole in the Gospel, written by Richard Stearns. It was given to us at the precise time we needed to see it, and it instantly spoke to our hearts. It confirmed that our next adventure was part of God's plan for our lives. In the book, Stearns shares how the founder of World Vision, Bob Pierce, prayed, "Let my heart be broken with the things that break the heart of God." [7] This was an impactful question for me to reflect on and eventually act on. It enlightened us to a world that we conceptually knew existed but didn't begin to understand. It was the first step in opening our eyes to the world we were meant to see and experience. A world that would allow our hearts to break in a new way and create a desire we never knew lived inside us.

Early into our first trip to Uganda, Dave and I knew that our purpose in being there was bigger than our adoption. We knew that now that our eyes were open, it would be impossible to walk away and never look back. Every day we were in Uganda, our lives

---

[7] Richard Stearns. *The Hole in the Gospel*. (Nashville, Tennessee, W Publishing, an imprint of Thomas Nelson, 2009), xxix.

were changing. We were in the company of unbelievably spirit-filled people who carried a faith and a joy like we had never seen. Others, however, did not possess this joy and were in desperate need.

Two years after coming home, we started our non-profit, Kuyamba Ministries. Kuyamba means "to help" in Luganda. For years, Livingstone, now with his wife Anna, has led a team that goes into villages every Saturday. They bring supplies to help people with whatever needs they may have. They take hygiene, first aid supplies, and food to share with the people they meet. Their goal is to meet the person's physical need and, while doing so, share Jesus with them. Their main goal is to love people, show them that someone cares, and, most importantly, share Jesus.

For the first several years of Kuyamba, we served from afar, raising money and sending supplies to our dedicated team in Uganda. Many things were happening in our lives that prevented us from returning with Dave's eye surgeries. We knew God's plans involved just that, though. Eventually, we were back where we belonged to serve in person.

On one of our first days back in Uganda while on a mission, we found ourselves standing in front of a small church in the middle of a crowded village called Katogo. It was dark inside the small building constructed of some wooden boards and nails. The room overflowed with people from the village that had gathered because we had come to feed and share supplies with them. Our team in Uganda had been serving this village for over five years, visiting with them frequently. The conditions of this village are extremely poor, the poorest we have encountered. It was the rainy season, and mud filled the walkways. On either side were houses built with sticks and mud, with perhaps some aluminum roofing if they were lucky. With the rain, these houses eventually crumble, and they will find themselves rebuilding them. They will sleep and put their children to bed at night, knowing that the rain will make its way through at some point.

Our team had prepared a meal of rice and meat to serve the village that evening. We filled about 500 plastic bags of food to distribute. Afterward, we would share the other supplies and talk to people to learn about their needs. As we began to hand out the bags of food to the kids up front, a few mothers approached me and knelt at my feet, sharing their needs with me and asking for my help. I could not understand everything they were saying, so someone from our team would help translate as needed. Many of them said they needed better roofing to keep the rain out. Others asked for help for their children because they were sick or hungry. Several women approached me and would fall to their knees, believing I would have the answers. I was overwhelmed with emotion, desperate for answers as to how this could be their reality.

After some time, I found a little space. I stood there alone and looked out at the crowd. I was overcome. I knew the needs, we'd been sending supplies, and our team was doing missions every weekend. But now, we were in person, looking into their eyes face-to-face and seeing the world they face every day. I have never been so humbled.

The reality of it all fell on me hard and quick. For several minutes, I felt utterly lost, crying for these people. I looked at their faces, thinking they shouldn't have to live like this. They deserve better. While I would not have chosen to sit there and sob uncontrollably in front of everyone, that's what happened. God had me exactly where he wanted me. He wanted me to feel what I was feeling more profoundly than ever before. My heart was breaking for all the right reasons. God was fueling the fire inside.

When we started Kuyamba Ministries, we knew the needs were so great that we would never be able to take care of them all. We were searching our hearts to figure out our role in caring for others. We kept coming back to the idea of outreach in the villages, meeting people right where they were and providing some help. While doing that, we could pray and share Jesus. That passion had also been placed on Livingstone's heart many years before we met. We know we can't fix everything. Somehow, if we can meet one need for a person, we can then share God's love with them. Countless people have given their lives to Christ because of these outreaches. No one will ever have all of their needs met here on earth, whether that be a physical need or an emotional need. We do have the promise that we will need no more once we are with Him. Because of that, we will share God's love one person at a time. Our prayer is through Him; people's eternal needs will be met by accepting Jesus into their lives.

We felt God calling us to plant some roots on our first trip back. Part of that was finding a village where we could plant some seeds. Our team had scouted out some possible options before we arrived. We were seeking a place where we could reach several villages. There were several areas they wanted to show us. So off we went looking at land. Dave and I had absolutely no idea what we were actually looking for. How could we possibly know that one piece of land was better than another? Luckily, our friend Paul has experience in this and had done his homework before we arrived. Dave and I prepared to rely wholly on God to speak to us when we found the right spot. Like I had many times before, I prayed for God to speak as clearly as He possibly could to me because that is what I need. We looked at a few pieces of land and didn't feel anything. We knew we had not arrived at the right place yet. We drove some more, and as we turned a corner to a new site, something started stirring in me. I couldn't explain it and kept it to myself. We made our way down a small lane and parked the van. I got out and took a few steps ahead of the others. I tried to let it sink in, but I quickly stopped in my tracks. I turned around and said – this is it! Dave immediately said the same. He had the same feeling inside him as we drove down the lane. Even blind, he felt the Holy Spirit telling him this was the place. I might as well have been blind because I had no idea what I was looking at either. I was ultimately going off the stirring of the Holy Spirit inside of me. God had answered our prayer and made it clear to us that this was the place.

We go through many of our days wondering if we are doing the right thing or making the right decision. Our minds are filled with noise from the world we live in. Most days, we have so much going on that we forget that our answers are a prayer away. In the quietness of that field, we felt God speak to us. It was awesome to experience that clarity from Him. What an important lesson as we go through our day-to-day lives. We must make sure we allow the quietness so we can hear from Him.

We made an offer on the land that day, and it was ours.

Actually, it is His, and we get to borrow it. This little village, Wabukwa, resides near a market area with a lot of traffic. Paul had done his research and knew we would be able to pull water to this site and electricity when the time came. We dream of constructing a multipurpose building on this land that will serve as a feeding center, medical clinic, STEM robotics educational center, and most importantly, a church. It will be the Kuyamba Community Center because we really want it to be that, a place where villagers can gather that is their own.

In the shorter term, we have built a latrine on the land. The government requires that a latrine be the first thing built in an area where people will gather. We were so proud of that little latrine. People sometimes look at me funny when I show them pictures and ask if they agree it is the cutest little latrine they've ever seen. We have also built a pavilion where the village can gather and start meeting for church. We will also construct a large outdoor kitchen and a large playground for the children to enjoy. As I stood on that land that day, with banana trees, maize, and a wide variety of prickly grasses, I knew God had big plans for this little piece of land.

A couple of days later, we spent a day going home to home in this area. The simplest way to explain what it felt like was that we were home. I can only imagine all of the preparations God pulls together and lines up for His people so that things come together as He wants them to.

The people were warm and welcoming as we traveled through the village. Even though we could not understand each other well, we shared smiles and many hugs. As we reached a home where no one was outside, our team told us that the woman who lived there had a stroke and was inside. We found ourselves around the back of the house and went through a small doorway. They lead us to her. Her name was Mary. She sat in a chair by the one small window in the front room. There was another woman there who was her caretaker. As I approached her, I leaned over and reached my hand to hers. She grabbed hold of my hand tightly. She could not speak. She caught my eyes as we looked at each other, and we stayed like that for some time. She smiled back as I smiled at her, still holding my hand. I thought about what she had been through, where she now sits, likely for the remainder of her days. I looked at one of our team members beside me and asked, "does she know Jesus?" I looked back at her, and she smiled again. With her other hand, she made a cross over her heart. It was hard for me to walk away from her that day. The Holy Spirit was working in Mary, and I was the recipient. I will never forget that brief time I spent holding Mary's hand and looking into her eyes, talking with no words as if we were souls meant to meet. Experiences like these stir the fire inside me, reminding me of what I am fighting for. It also brings me to the realization that only God could have brought me here.

On our last trip to Uganda, we were in a small, remote village that had never had a missionary visit. They welcomed us so graciously. They prepared food, music, and dances for us. I was in awe of what they had prepared for us. They sat us in the front row as they played drums, sang songs, worshiped, and danced. As I sat there, I thought, how in the world am I sitting in this far-off village, on this particular day, experiencing these beautiful people at this very moment? Knowing on the other side of the world, people are busily living their lives without a thought about what is happening where I am. I felt how special it was that God chose me to be there. The little girl from Indiana who never wanted to leave home was comfortable on the other side of the world. I felt more alive than ever, having to pinch myself to understand this was real. I have been to some beautiful places in my life, but none compare to the people we have met across the globe.

I would have laughed if anyone had told me ten years ago that I would find myself in an empty field in Uganda, ready to say yes to planting roots in this far away land. Going to Uganda was never on my list. It was so far beyond what I could envision that it would never have crossed my mind. We are so fortunate to have a God that is willing and capable of pulling us outside of our own world. Going to Uganda is the hardest thing that I have ever done. But at the same time, it's the best and most adventurous thing I have ever done. It's a place that makes me feel things I didn't know I would ever feel. It's a place that gives me the courage to fight.

Our Mission Is On. The title of this chapter is just that. Many Fridays, Livingstone will post on Facebook, Our Mission Is On. Every outreach they do, they call a mission. It's the perfect description, really. They are on a mission to serve. More than anything, they are on a mission for lost souls.

> *2 Corinthians 3:3 says, "You show that you are a letter from Christ, the result of our ministry, written not with ink but with the Spirit of the living God, not on tablets of stone but on the tablets of human hearts."*

I can't think of a more important mission than that.

SIXTEEN

Finding My Way Home

Jesus answered, "I am the way and the truth and the life. No one comes to the Father except through me."

—John 14:6

I am honored that you have taken this journey with me.

When I think of home, I see myself approaching a door. When I envision the door I will reach at the end of my time on this Earth, it is worn. The paint is peeling; it's endured a few storms. Even so, my door is beautiful. It's not perfect, yet it is warm and inviting; it has character and charm. And—it's still standing!

While working on this project, I pictured a door on the front of this book. It looked much like the one I described above. It wasn't until I was finished telling my story that I started to see the long and winding road it takes to get there. It's the long walk home that shapes us and prepares us to open that door when we finally reach our destination. Until then, I continue to follow His path as I find my way home.

God never promised this life would be easy. He promised to walk with us, even carry us when needed. I can even picture God dragging me (in the most loving way) when I was kicking and screaming my way through life, reminding me it would be okay.

While waiting to bring Fiona home, I connected with a long-distance friend who sent me encouraging messages regularly. I always looked forward to what she would have to say. One day she told me if I could not face the day, I needed to climb up on

God's big lap and let Him hold me. Some days, we need to take the time to do just that.

I started this book by talking about a favorite Casting Crowns song, I Am Yours. Another song by them, Just Be Held, has also come to have significant meaning to me. There is one line in particular that I have held onto and recalled when life has been challenging. It says, "If your eyes are on the storm, you'll wonder if I love you still, but if your eyes are on the cross, you'll know I always have, and I always will." [8]

I have listened to this song countless times. These words remind me where to focus – the cross. When the storm is too fierce, the best thing we can do is let go and be held. Let God work. I must share the good news because of what He has done for me. You are the reason I answered His call to share my story.

"I have told you these things, so that in me you may have peace. In this world, you will have trouble. But, take heart! I have overcome the world." John 16:33

I love this scripture. It is a scripture I go to often in times of trouble or worry. Yes, there will be trouble. But take heart. God has overcome this world. We can't do it alone, and God doesn't want us to. Why do we often think we have to overcome trouble on our own? God invites us to involve Him in our lives – every last little detail. He wants to fight our battles, he wants to provide us strength, and he wants to walk with us. And the beautiful thing is if we allow ourselves to open up to Him, anything is possible. Things we thought we could never handle, we can with Him.

---

[8] Mark Hall, Matthew West and Bernie Helms, "Just Be Held," Provident Music Distribution, 2014.

The world wants us to think there are answers all around to fix us. It fools us into thinking things other than God will fill our hearts. While the world may try to complicate Christianity, it does not have to be. Jesus loves all people, and he wants everyone to know that truth. I can't promise you an easy life if you choose Jesus. It may not even be the easy choice. I know that if you do, you will find hope and peace because you will learn that by choosing Him, you are choosing to trust and believe in something more than this world will ever give you. You won't be able to physically see it, but you will feel it, and it will become your greatest possession.

I'm still finding my way home. I don't know what the next chapter, or what the several after that, will look like. I don't know what roads I'm going to take, which way I'll have to turn. My gas tank may not always be full. I don't know what is ahead, but I know it will be filled with laughter. I know it will be full of twists and turns I could never anticipate. I know with Him it will be exciting and adventurous. When you let Him lead, it's going to be amazing! I know there will be times life will be filled with tears and sadness. I know that in my imperfection, there will be times I don't want to endure something life throws at me, and I will ask Him why. I learned a long time ago that we can't try to hide our feelings from Him because He is all-knowing. And thankfully, He loves us all the same. We are human. He created us knowing our strengths and weaknesses and loves us regardless.

Every single one of us is His child. I think that is the best title I could have in this world. As a parent, I know how much I love my children and how my heart is whole when they are safely home with me. God is the same. There is nothing He wants more at the end of our time than for us to come home. He has called us to be His disciples in this world, and His desire is that we will bring others to Him. I know where I am going. I am finding my way home. That is what I want for you, too.

My prayer is for you to fully accept Jesus as your Lord and Savior; surrender your past and your pain to Him trusting He will take care of it. I pray that you find your strength and confidence in Him alone. My prayer is for you to find peace in Him. I pray for all of this, knowing it is entirely possible because I have discovered these things through Him alone.

God doesn't want you to walk alone. He sent His own Son to come into this world and walk beside us. That is why He allowed that one and only Son to bear the sin of this world and die on a cross to free us so that we can live a life of eternity with Him. When I look at the cross, I see it as the greatest expression of God's love for us. God wants to provide you a way to live in this world, to be His. You already are. He has felt your hurt and pain, and He wants you to walk into His open arms so that you can feel the love he has to offer.

Accept the greatest gift of all time. The Savior in a manger was sent to save this world. God's greatest gift. Wrapped simply yet beautifully, just for you.

"For God so loved the world, that he gave his only Son,
that whoever believes in him should not
perish but have eternal life."
— John 3:16

ACKNOWLEDGMENTS

Dave, thank you for allowing me to share our story. Thank you for loving me just as I am. For the strength you have shown me when I needed it the most. For relentlessly pushing me to take the next leap of faith and finish this book. For praying for me constantly. For always believing in me. Thank you for taking those vows, for better or worse, and bringing them to life. While neither of us would say it's been easy, we are living our vows each day and deciding to continue this journey together. I love you.

Tyler, I want you to know you are loved more than you could ever know. Something you will understand when you have kids of your own. You are fierce, a force to be reckoned with. You are bold, determined, and bright, and you dream big. I've known since the instant you came into this world that you would do big things. While you are forever mine, I want you to always know who you belong to. I want you to live life fully with God at the center. I want you to always keep Him close to your heart and hang onto the cross. While I would never try to take credit for the man you've become, you are still one of my greatest accomplishments. Because of you, my heart learned the meaning of unconditional love.

Fiona, thank you for allowing me to share your story. You are so brave. From the moment I met you in that curtain-draped doorway to waiting for me to return not once but twice to bring you home – you continue to amaze me. I know you have heard me say this a million times, but you are my living, breathing, answered prayer that dances before my eyes each day. You are a constant reminder to me of God's love and grace. Your heart for others is big and beautiful. It is an honor to watch you take on the world and find your voice and God's purpose. I know you can't yet envision what you will do, but you will shine and bring joy to whatever that is. You are intelligent in all the right ways, creative and artistic, fierce and funny simultaneously, and so much more. Always know who you belong to. I am so proud to call you my daughter.

To my parents and my incredible family, thank you for always being there for us. You have taken care of us during our illnesses and trials. You have bravely allowed us to travel across the world (many times now) to fulfill God's calling in our lives. I know it was never easy to let us go. You have picked up the pieces and filled the holes to make this all work. Thank you for believing in us, walking with us, and praying for us. I can't imagine living this life without each of you in it.

Friends, who we are blessed to have in abundance, thank you for loving us and for your endless prayers. Whether you are near or far, thank you for choosing to live life with us. Thank you for always being there, whatever the need. We are blessed beyond measure by each of you.

To our friends who are now family in Uganda, thank you for welcoming us into your world and adopting us as your own. You have taught us how to be disciples in this world. Your relentless pursuit to share God's love with others inspires us. Thank you for your prayers that never cease.

To new friends gained through sharing my testimony, I look forward to walking with you and hearing your stories.

BIBLIOGRAPHY

Boltz, Raymond H. *Thank You*. Track 2 on Thank You. Steve Millikan, Word Distribution, 1994, compact disc.

Cox, Sidney E. *Deep and Wide*. Ruth P. Overholtzer in Salvation Songs for Children No. Three, 1947.

Hall, Mark, Matthew West and Bernie Helms, "Just Be Held," Provident Music Distribution, 2014, compact disc.

Hall, Mark. "Who Am I." Track 4 on *Casting Crowns*. Mark A Hall and Steven Curtis Chapman. Provident Music Distribution, 2003, compact disc.

Lemmel, Helen H. *Turn Your Eyes Upon Jesus*. Glad Songs. British National Sunday School Union, 1922.

Spafford, Horatio. *It Is Well With My Soul*. Bliss and Sankey, Gospel Hymns No. 2, 1876.

Stearns, Richard. *The Hole in the Gospel*. Nashville, Tennessee, an imprint of Thomas Nelson, 2009.

Fifty percent of proceeds for Finding My Way Home will go to Kuyamba Ministries.

For more information, you may go to www.kuyambaministries.com or www.sarabennettbrodzinski.com